"IF THE GOSPEL IS TRUE, WHY DO I HURT SO MUCH?"

CARROLL HOFELING MORRIS

"IF THE GOSPEL IS TRUE, WHY DO I HURT SO MUCH?"

HELP FOR DYSFUNCTIONAL LATTER-DAY SAINT FAMILIES

Deseret Book Company
Salt Lake City, Utah

Excerpt from *For Your Own Good* by Alice Miller. Copyright (©) 1983 by Alice Miller. Reprinted by permission of Farrar, Straus and Giroux, Inc.

Reprinted with the permission of the publishers Health Communications, Inc., Deerfield Beach, Florida, from *Adult Children of Alchoholics,* by Janet G. Woititz, Ed.D., copyright date 1983.

Excerpts from *Becoming Your Own Parent* by Dennis Wholely are reprinted with permission of Doubleday, a division of Bantam, Doubleday, Dell Publishing Group, Inc., copyright (©) 1988.

Library of Congress Cataloging-in-Publication Data

Morris, Carroll Hofeling.
    If the Gospel is true, why do I hurt so much? : help for dysfunctional LDS families / Carroll Hofeling Morris.
        p.   cm.
    Includes bibliographical references and index.
    ISBN 0-87579-539-0
    1. Church work with families — Mormon Church.   2. Problem families.
I. Title.
BX8643.F3M75   1992
248.4'89332 — dc20   91-28889
                                                                      CIP

Printed in the United States of America
10   9   8   7   6   5   4   3   2   1

For the members of my family,
who have spent many years
beside me in the trenches

CONTENTS

CONTENTS

ACKNOWLEDGMENTS

The help and support of many people made the preparation of this manuscript easier. Eleanor Knowles and Sheri Dew of Deseret Book Company encouraged me to develop my idea for the book, which was quite different from the fiction I have written in the past. Alan R. Anderson, Ph.D., and Roger K. Allen, Ph.D., offered their professional expertise in the area of family theory and family therapy. My sister Nancy Anderson, who was involved in every stage of the project, contributed immensely. She helped with the research and edited an early version of the manuscript, suggesting many improvements in both style and content. And Richard Tice, my editor at Deseret Book, did his usual excellent job at identifying areas needing improvement. And while I may complain during the revision process, I'm always pleased with the result. A special thanks goes to my family, who ate a leaning tower's worth of pizza when I was too busy to cook — and never complained!

CLARIFICATION OF TERMS

I have used the term *dysfunctional* throughout this book because it is a common and generally accepted term that means impaired or abnormal functioning. However, I agree with those experts who point out that families with the kinds of problems described in this book all function in some fashion. They may, for example, alternate periods of dysfunction or chaos with periods of quiet.

Another frequently used term is *adult children*. It describes individuals who grew up in dysfunctional families. The complete phrase as found in literature on the subject is *adult children of dysfunctional families*. The expression refers to the fact that such individuals are trapped in negative behavior patterns they developed in childhood as a way of coping with their family situations. Thus, although they are physically mature adults, they can be thought of as children in the sense that they have not matured beyond childhood in some important aspects.

In the second half of the book, I discuss the *inner child*. You will notice that I often refer to the inner child with the pronouns *she* and *her*. I do this because some traits often thought of as particularly feminine are associated with the inner child, including vulnerability and openness to emotions and intuition.

These are *not* exclusively feminine traits, however, and all references to the inner child apply equally to men and women.

You may also notice that stories or statistics in the sections on abuse seem weighted toward females. This is a reflection of two facts. First, women are more often the victims of abuse than men. Second, not as much information is available concerning men and abuse. As you read these sections, please remember that there are male victims as well as female victims, and both are struggling with the same issues. Male victims have the same need for support and healing.

Finally, as you read the book, you may experience a *recognition response*, signalled by an inner click, an AHA! moment or a shift in awareness. The recognition response is a clear indication that some part of what you are reading is true for you. If that should happen, I encourage you to pursue an understanding of the issue involved and seek the help, should it be necessary, to work it out.

INTRODUCTION

Some years ago, the stake president spoke to my ward the Sunday before Christmas. What he told us that day came as a surprise, for it wasn't the expected reflection on the season. He said: "Some of you may have noticed my eyes fill with tears during this service, and you may have concluded they were the result of my being moved by the Christmas message. That is not the case. They were the result of my looking out into your faces and seeing so much pain."

My husband, Gary, and I were among those whose faces did not express the joy of the season. At that time — and for many years thereafter — we were caught in a destructive cycle. The harder we tried to do everything we thought the Church and the gospel required, the less joy, comfort, peace, and family unity we experienced. Feelings of shame and low self-esteem followed. The gospel seemed to be working in other peoples' lives, so why wasn't it working in ours?

Our response was to try harder, to do more, to suppress negative feelings. Sooner or later, we thought, we would do it right. Then everything would be the way it was supposed to be. Our efforts didn't bring us the desired results, however. They didn't address the prime difficulty, which lay in the nature of our

1

family relationships. We didn't know it at the time, but we were what professionals call a dysfunctional family.

In the years since that Christmas Sunday, I have learned that in order to be set free, we need to know certain truths in addition to those set forth in the scriptures — truths specific to our own lives. For example, we who grew up in dysfunctional families or are presently in dysfunctional relationships need to

- face the truth about the nature of those relationships.
- learn the truth about the survival techniques and ways of relating to others that we adopted in the past — and what effect they have on our lives in the present.
- truly experience rather than deny our feelings, those associated with both childhood and present events.
- make an honest commitment to do the work necessary for healing and growth, both as individuals and as families.

These tasks cannot be ignored, for dysfunction profoundly affects individuals and families. It gives rise to destructive beliefs about the nature of God, man, and relationships, which in turn reinforce destructive behavior patterns. Negative beliefs and behavior patterns both create difficulties in relationships and blunt the individual's ability to understand the Atonement and partake of its transforming power. They thus block spiritual growth.

Judging from my own experience and the experience of others, members of dysfunctional families often do not recognize what is impeding their spiritual progress. They try to solve their problems by putting increased energy into church activities while leaving the underlying causes unaddressed. In this case, the kind of improvement in spirituality and relationships they long for will remain outside their grasp.

However, when new understanding of relationship principles is combined with self-examination, positive changes can occur, not only in family life, but also in spiritual life. For as our un-

2

derstanding of correct relationship principles and our ability to live by them increase, our understanding of gospel principles and our ability to live by them also increase. Understanding the principles of relationships is thus a necessary part of working out our salvation.

My own efforts in this direction took many paths. I read through piles of current literature on dysfunctional families. I attended seminars. I meditated and prayed. I talked to Church leaders and to men and women who had similar problems, many of whom expressed great relief at being able to discuss openly the difficulties they were facing.

As a writer, I felt compelled to put all that I had learned into a meaningful form. *If the Gospel Is True, Why Do I Hurt So Much?* is the result. There is nothing unusual about the information presented in the book—it is a synthesis of the most important messages I gleaned from numerous sources. However, because of the personal (rather than scholarly) nature of the book, I didn't hesitate to interpret what I had learned in the context of my experience as an LDS woman. That is unusual. Although material on dysfunctional families and codependency fills a large space in most bookstores, little has been previously written presenting these issues from an LDS viewpoint.

Many Latter-day Saints living in dysfunctional families were willing not only to share their experiences with me, but also to allow me to include those experiences in the book. I hope this is an early signal that a new openness is developing among us about the realities many face. Such openness need not be feared. It neither attacks the Church nor indicts those experiencing difficulties. As John Bradshaw, leading authority on dysfunctional families, has said, "Everyone is responsible, but no one is to blame."[1] By taking responsibility for our roles in a painful family system, we take the first step in healing.

3

PART 1
THE PROBLEM

CHAPTER 1

CONFRONTING THE ISSUE

Nothing is so painful as realizing the gap between what can be and what is. That realization is especially painful in regard to family life. For members of The Church of Jesus Christ of Latter-day Saints who are experiencing difficult relationships, unresolved conflict, or abuse, it is bitterly painful.

We belong to a church that puts commitment to family second only to commitment to Christ. We have been taught that if we live the principles of the gospel, enter into the ordinances, and keep the outward observances, we will have happy, successful families. Unfortunately, that is not always the case. Faithfully doing Church work, for example, doesn't compensate for lack of knowledge about how relationships work — or lack of effort toward making them work.

When President Benson exhorted Church members to read the Book of Mormon as families and promised them blessings if they would, my husband and I renewed our efforts to get our children together for morning scripture reading. I recall a week when we actually read the Book of Mormon seven days out of seven! However, that accomplishment did not provide us with the tools we needed to understand and resolve our family difficulties. And the fact that we were obedient to President Benson's call, yet failed to improve our situation, added to our burden of sorrow and frustration.

Church members who are striving unsuccessfully to create a "forever family" feel separated from those whose family lives are healthy and happy. They are plagued by grave doubts about themselves and the Church. They listen with heavy hearts to testimonies, to missionary farewell speeches, and to Mother's and Father's Day talks. The words of hope, love, and happiness seem directed to everyone else but them.

Imagine, if you are not one of those suffering because of acute family problems, what it must feel like to be a Church member in the following situations:

> 1
> The children in Primary are singing "I'm so glad when daddy comes home . . . " Mark sits with his shoulders slumped, swinging his feet back and forth. He doesn't feel like singing along because he isn't glad when his daddy gets home. His daddy is always mad at something. Mark has to be very careful to do everything right because if he doesn't . . .
> Mark doesn't like to sing "I Am a Child of God" either, because God hasn't given him parents kind and dear. He often wonders why. Is it because God doesn't love him? Or because he's bad?
>
> 2
> Jennifer's Laurel teacher is talking about the joys of marriage and motherhood. The minute she begins, Jennifer focuses on a corner of the ceiling and tunes out. She's heard it all a hundred times before, and frankly she doesn't believe it anymore. She's seen too much conflict between her parents, some of it violent. She doesn't get along with her siblings, either. *This happy family stuff*, she thinks, *is either a big lie, or it's only for some people. I'm obviously not*

8

one of them. She has long since given up on the idea of a temple marriage.

3

Milly bites her lip to keep from crying as she listens to a Relief Society sister tell about how her prayers for a wayward daughter brought the daughter back into the fold of the family and the Church. Milly also has a daughter who has chosen a way of life contrary to the principles of the gospel. Milly has prayed for her daughter night and day for many months. Her heart aches as she wonders why her prayers are not as effectual as those of the other sister.

4

George has begun to skip his priesthood quorum meetings. He doesn't feel comfortable among the other brethren, who seem to have no difficulty in leading and directing their families as heads of their households. George's wife has never respected his opinions, much less deferred to him as the priesthood holder in the family. His children have followed her example, showing him little respect. Whenever he attempts to present family goals to them, they resist. That makes him angry, and he ends up losing control. He hears over and over that he should be guiding his family toward celestial goals, so the fact that he has had so little success strikes at the root of his self-esteem. He feels he has failed as a husband and a father. He feels as if he is no good to his family or the Church — or even himself.

The fact that members in these and similar situations feel different or less worthy adds another level of pain to already painful circumstances. Some even feel that they are totally to blame for the unhappiness they are experiencing and that they are therefore inadequate. Others entertain grave doubts about their spirituality or the love of God for them. Such feelings are more pronounced if they felt that they were prompted in their choice of a mate but that the choice has led to a life fraught with anguish. As a result, they may become bitter and angry at God. Finding it increasingly difficult to believe that membership in the Church results in a better life, they begin to waver in their testimonies.

Such feelings of separation and doubt make continued Sabbath attendance and participation in Church activities difficult. Attending church is anything but a joyful experience if we are convinced that others would be shocked at what goes on within the walls of our homes. It is anything but a joyful experience if we feel as if we are living a lie—smiling on the outside while filled with anger, overwhelming grief, or depression on the inside.

I am not the only one whose Sunday smile covering everyday grief wore thin and then finally disappeared. No matter where you look, if you look beyond the surface signs, you will find families in pain. You will find them living in your stake, in your ward. Perhaps you visit or home teach them. Perhaps you belong to one of them.

We gain nothing by clinging to the illusion that if we pretend all is well in Zion, it will be so. The time has come for us to acknowledge the difficulties we and many of our fellow Saints are experiencing. The time has come to search for answers to the questions that so many of us ask as we lie awake in the dark:

What went wrong?

How can we make it right?

CHAPTER 2

WHERE WE ARE NOW

At the end of the movie *Raising Arizona*, the main character has a dream in which he sees the figures of an old woman and an old man surrounded by their posterity. He says, "It seemed real. It seemed like us, like . . . well, our home. If not Arizona, then a land not too far away, where all parents are strong and wise and capable, and all children are happy and beloved. . . . I don't know. Maybe it was Utah."

That line is good for a laugh—and a few tears. That's the way we wish it were, not only in Utah, but in the stakes of Zion wherever they are. But all is not well in Utah, and all is not well in Zion. More subtle kinds of dysfunction aside, the concern of the brethren over the level of abuse in LDS families is proof enough. One indicator of this concern can be found in the fact that a specific question regarding abuse is now asked in temple recommend interviews. Another is the talks and writings of General Authorities on the subject.

In an article entitled "Unrighteous Dominion," Elder H. Burke Peterson wrote:

> The letters and phone calls the Brethren receive
> from faithful wives and children who are emotion-

11

ally and physically abused in their homes continue to multiply. . . . Countless heartaches and mis-shaped lives result from this unrighteous behav-ior. . . .

It may be relatively mild when expressed as crit-icism, anger, or feelings of severe frustration. In more extreme cases, however, unrighteous domin-ion may emerge as verbal, physical, or emotional abuse. Unfortunately, in its less obvious forms, un-righteous dominion is often either ignored or not recognized as such.[1]

Although Brother Peterson was speaking of men as abusers, his words can also apply to women and even children. In par-ticular, abuse by siblings is often ignored or passed over with comments such as, "That's just the ways kids act at that age," or "It's not unusual for brothers and sisters to squabble."

The last part of the Peterson quotation is of great importance. Some actions and attitudes that we consider normal to family life are actually abusive. Anne L. Horton, assistant professor in Brigham Young University's School of Social Work, has enum-erated some of the more subtle forms of abuse.[2] I have listed them below, along with some additions:

Physical

- poking, prodding, shoving
- hair-pulling
- hard, prolonged tickling
- intense wrestling

Psychological/emotional

- name-calling, using sarcasm, making biting comments
- insulting, yelling, swearing, threatening
- criticizing
- manipulating, guilting, shaming, gossiping
- withholding of affection, attention, or respect

12

- withholding of help, making false promises
- lying, withholding information
- using money as a lever to get what you want
- making fun of or rejecting others' thoughts, feelings, or needs

Sexual

- inappropriate touching, hugging, kissing
- invading privacy
- making crude or sexist comments, telling sexual jokes
- taking inordinate interest in private matters

This is a sobering list, for I believe if readers honestly contemplate it, they will recognize some of their own behaviors.

Abuse is pervasive, as shown by national statistics. In 1989, an estimated 2,400,000 children were reported to have been abused or neglected. This represents a ten percent increase over the reported incidents filed in 1988.[3] An article in *Psychology Today* reported that one in six Americans is sexually abused as a child, or twenty-five percent of all females and ten percent of all males.[4] Other studies put the figure even higher for men. *Newsweek* reported that there was some form of violence in twenty-five percent of American marriages.[5]

Members of the Church often feel that because we have the blessing of the restored gospel, we also have — or ought to have — some immunity from the relationship problems faced by the population as a whole, including abuse. However, this does not seem to be the case. Although there are few available statistis relating directly to physical and sexual abuse among the LDS population, the studies that have been done allow us to draw some conclusions.

Projections by the YWCA women's shelter program indicate that in 1991, 57,630 Utah men will assault a domestic partner. In other words, one of ten Utah women will be assaulted by a

domestic partner. Furthermore, 144,470 Utah children will witness violence between their parents or between their mothers
and partners. Seventy-two thousand will suffer assault as well.

The YWCA statistics also indicate that of the Utah children
reared in violent and abusive homes, 65% (approximately
93,650) will marry into abusive family systems. Unless they receive or seek help to break the cycle, they in turn will produce
234,120 children who will be reared in abusive homes, 65% of
whom, if the patterns are not altered, will marry into abusive
family systems.[6]

While these statistics do not indicate the number of Latter-
day Saints living in Utah who might be affected by domestic
violence, the high percentage of Church members in the Utah
population (an estimated 77.2% in 1991–1992) makes them per-
tinent to any discussion on dysfunction in an LDS context.

A study on violence in Utah County that compared results
with a national study was also revealing.[7] According to the research, spanking occurs at a ten percent higher rate in Utah
County than the national average (82% national, 93% Utah
County). In addition, half of the parents stated that if they saw
someone do to their children the sorts of things they themselves
did, they would call the police!

These results were echoed in the study "In Search of a Peculiar
People: Are Mormons Really Different?"[8] Statistics from the 1987
National Survey of Families and Households were used to compare
LDS families with several other religious groups. Again, the
percentages of spanking, slapping, or yelling incidents among
Latter-day Saints were slightly, though not significantly, higher.
(A possible explanation is the greater number of small children
in LDS families than the national average.)

Reference was also made in the above study to an analysis
of violence in a Utah sample by Rollins and Oheneba-Sakyi.[9]
That analysis "indicates that spousal violence is slightly more

14

common in Utah than in the United States. Utah households report a little less violence toward children than U.S. households, but violence is more likely among women if they have a college degree, but do not work, or if they have sole responsibility for child care."

On the basis of such studies and her own practice dealing with victims of abuse, Anne Horton concludes that LDS families have the same risk for physical, sexual, or emotional abuse as any other social group. In fact, she estimates that two million Latter-day Saints will have been abused by the year 2000.

There will be other victims too. Family members who witness the incidents can be added to the count. And because abuse victims often in turn abuse others, the number will continue to rise.

If we are to reverse this trend, we must begin to educate ourselves and to develop the systems necessary to offer appropriate help. Now is the time to begin. As Anne Horton remarked in the 1990 BYU Women's Conference, "These topics are not too awful to mention, they are too critical and awful not to mention. Now may not be a comfortable time to solve or face this problem, but it is the only time."[10]

CHAPTER 3

BELIEFS THAT KEEP US
FROM GETTING HELP

Many of us judge our success by how happy our family life is. It doesn't seem to matter what we have accomplished or what acclaim we have received; if our relationships are troubled, we feel as if we have failed. Not surprisingly, then, we want to believe our families are normal, happy, and healthy; that our relationships are free of dysfunction.

The fact is, most of us either have experienced or are experiencing some level of dysfunction in some relationship. We may not recognize it as such, however, especially if it is subtle or if we don't clearly understand what sorts of behavior are dysfunctional. We may actually be tolerating some physical, verbal, or emotional abuse, believing the myth that it is a normal part of family life.

False Measures of Family Success

In addition, we often define family success on the basis of externals. But what makes a family dysfunctional is not always visible to outsiders. Family members may seem to be normal and happy. They may live in a comfortable home. They may be high achievers or leaders in Church and society. They may be all of that, and their families may still be dysfunctional.

Let's take a close look at three typical criteria for success to see how misleading they can be: absence of overt conflict, activity in the Church, and financial and social success.

Absence of conflict. The level of overt conflict alone isn't an accurate measuring stick for dysfunction. When we believe that lack of conflict is an indication of good relationships, we do all we can to avoid or minimize disagreements or fights, thinking that to do so is the way to make our families successful.

If the individual's need for safety, respect, love, and encouragement are met, the presence of conflict per se does not appear to have lasting detrimental effects. Problems are resolved in ways that do not shame the individual or cause him to doubt his worth.

On the other hand, when absence of conflict is made into the measuring stick, the means used to avoid it are often in themselves abusive or manipulative and result in future relationship difficulties. Some examples are acknowledging that a problem exists but refusing to talk about it, denying that a problem exists, making fun of the individual's concerns or fears, and withholding love or approval until the individual conforms to expectations. Those who believe that any means of avoiding open conflict is justified in the effort to build a strong family unit are often unhappily surprised at the results, as was Ann in the following anecdote.

Many times, Ann* heard her mother and father say with pride that they had never had an argument in all their married life. It was true. Differences of opinion, anger, and frustration were never articulated—that was the family rule. When she married, Ann held fast to that rule and avoided talking about

---

*The names and nonessential circumstances in true-life examples have been changed.

17

negative feelings, believing that the absence of conflict indicated a well-balanced family.

On the surface, her relationship with her husband looked fine, but the resulting lack of communication became so severe and disabling that it eventually led to a divorce. Now Ann is struggling to learn how to acknowledge negative feelings, particularly anger, and to face and work out conflict in an appropriate manner.

Activity in the Church. While activity in the Church does support parents in their goals and contribute to the strength of the family, it is not a guarantee against dysfunction. Members of a dysfunctional family can attend all their meetings, pay tithing, support a missionary, obey the Word of Wisdom, read scriptures regularly, and fill various positions in their ward—and still be at the mercy of destructive relationship patterns. In fact, dysfunctional families often become overly involved in Church activities as a means of avoiding unpleasant family issues. Family members will continue to have problems until they deal with the issues that are causing them pain.

The Webers were a pillar of their ward. A large family, they filled positions of prominence and attended all ward functions. The children were lively yet well-mannered and always well-groomed, and they received all of the expected awards as they passed through the Church organizations. They seemed to others to be good examples of family life.

However, there were problems at home. Brother Weber's parenting style was to give orders to his children, then have his wife see that they were carried out while he busied himself with business or Church work. Sister Weber, who herself was accustomed to receiving a list of "To Do's" from her husband, was unable to stand in as the authority figure in the family. The children routinely took advantage of their father's absence. Brother Weber would then upbraid his wife for not being able to control them. In turn, Sister Weber retaliated against her husband for being put into an unmanageable situation by sabotaging him in several ways, including always being late for important events, never having his shirts ironed when he needed them, and overdrawing the bank account.

Financial and social success. Given the affluence of our country and the emphasis on consumerism, we should not be surprised that many adults fall into the trap of basing their identities upon the goods they accumulate and the status they achieve. Success in worldly terms is extremely important to individuals who have no deep, anchoring sense of self-worth. In such cases, a spacious house with elegant furnishings immaculately kept, a luxury car, state-of-the-art electronic equipment, fashionable clothing, and a social life to match this life-style take on paramount importance. Relationships, even families, become adjuncts, props for the perfect picture.

Brother and Sister Lang were polished and educated. Both had grown up in favorable circumstances and had taken full advantage of the education and experiences offered them as a result. After twenty-five years of marriage, the Langs were living in the kind of home they had dreamed of, and they regularly took vacations to places with exotic names. Their children, all talented and smart, seemed to fit well into the structure of their lives.

However, both Brother and Sister Lang were emotionally remote people. They didn't know how to share their feelings, thoughts, and concerns in a significant way. The conversations they had with their children were more like corporate planning sessions, focused on logistics and problem-solving. Rarely were the children encouraged to talk about what they were experiencing, what they feared, what they hoped. By the time they reached their teenage years, the children no longer wanted to share significant aspects of their lives with their parents — their father and mother had a way of making them feel as if their

19

concerns were "no big deal." Emotions didn't matter. What mattered was that they lived up to the Lang image.

It was a great shock to the Langs when their teenage daughter committed suicide. When asked what might have been bothering their daughter, they couldn't say. In a very real way, she was a stranger to them. They listened with overwhelming grief and guilt as their other children revealed to them things they had never suspected about their daughter's life.

Often, men and women deny or don't recognize their family problems because of their focus on superficial standards of success. Men in particular may say things like, "I don't know what you're talking about when you say we have problems. What problems? I pay the bills. I do my Church work. I don't drink. I don't smoke. I don't go off with the guys on the weekend and leave you alone with the kids. You're the one with the problem. You're never satisfied."

On the other hand, when individuals are aware of family difficulties but are unable to effect positive change, they understandably often take comfort in the successes they achieve elsewhere. They may even put increased energy into jobs, volunteer work, or church work because they receive positive feedback for their efforts.

False Sense of Self-reliance

Quite a few families in pain often stay stuck because they believe in a false notion of self-reliance. They feel that they must *always* solve their family or personal problems without outside help. This attitude is particularly harmful because it supports the dysfunctional family's tendency to invalidate or reject information coming to them from the outside. Such families are what psychologists call "closed" systems.

The very fact that a dysfunctional family is a closed system precludes change. Unable or unwilling to see from a different viewpoint what is happening to them, they remain convinced that the way they perceive themselves, other family members, and their relationships with each other is correct. They may blame each other for their feelings of anger and pain, thus justifying their reactions. The cycle continues to replay over and over, the family members secure in the belief that they have good reason for their behavior.

In such a situation, *input from outside is necessary*, whether from counselors, friends, books, marriage retreats, or other sources. But even the suggestion of getting help can be perceived as a threat by family members who fear bringing the truth into the open.

A teenage girl from a troubled family was walking home from her music lesson one day when she noticed a new sign on a building: Family Counseling. She knew instinctively that family counseling was what she and her family needed. When she got home, she told her mother about the new service and suggested they check into it. The mother reacted as if she had been personally attacked, responding so negatively that the girl never brought up the subject again. But even as an adult, the daughter remembered that moment as a lost opportunity for change.

The idea that we can solve our problems on our own has the feeling of *hubris* about it. Usually used in context of Greek tragedy, hubris refers to impetuous or destructive behavior stemming from arrogance or excessive pride. The outcome is always disastrous in Greek drama and almost was in the following example.

An LDS woman was given an assignment by the Spiritual Living teacher to prepare a short talk on how learning to be self-reliant had helped her solve her family problems. She began her comments by remarking that she didn't think what she had to say was what the teacher wanted. She related that trying to solve the problems she and her family were facing without seeking outside help had led her perilously close to the ruin of her emotional health and the loss of her family.

This woman was born into a large farm family where the father saw sons as free labor and daughters as a waste of time and effort. Her earliest memory of her father was hearing him say that girls were no good and that she should have died at birth.

As can be imagined, hearing such emotionally and verbally abusive statements throughout her life created severe psychological problems that she was unable to resolve on her own. She tried to, however, by attempting to be the perfect Mormon wife and mother—but never dealing directly with the problem itself and never getting help (this kind of effort is described in chapter eleven in the discussion of codependence in LDS society). Doing so brought her family to the brink of disaster. She was only able to heal when she joined a 12-Step program dealing with codependence. It not only helped her understand what was at the root of her difficulties, but it also increased her spirituality by teaching her what it meant to be, as she put it, "God-reliant." That was when she and her family began to heal.

Fear of the Helping Profession

Many Church members also distrust the helping profession. Some seem to feel that those in the profession have rejected religious- or gospel-based values in favor of humanistic values or secular philosophies. This they see as a danger to the unity and strength of both the Church and the family. Those who believe in such sweeping generalizations do not acknowledge the resources available for families with problems, resources that they themselves may need.

Others may object to family members seeking help because they know that a reputable therapist will encourage his clients to express their feelings and decide for themselves what they

22

believe in and what they want. Some adults may see this as a threat to their authority as parents. Some husbands may see it as a threat to their position as head of the household. Some Church leaders may see it as a threat to the position that there is one inviolable, eternal standard of right and wrong.

Any time a family member enters some kind of therapy, the "family boat" is going to be rocked. The status quo will be upset. But that is exactly what closed, dysfunctional families need. The relationships must be changed; otherwise, such families cannot heal themselves. In addition, victims of any kind of abuse will need the help of a trained professional to work through the resulting problems.

The process of choosing a therapist to work with can allay some fears. Most services, like LDS Social Services and health maintenance organizations (HMOs), offer assistance in choosing counselors. Prospective clients should talk to various therapists and some of their current clients before making their choice. This can be done even when insurance coverage limits the choice of therapists to those within a specific group health plan. And if clients find they are uncomfortable with their first choice of therapists, they can always change.

Fear of Admitting Failure

Finally, many people don't seek help because they don't see a problem, even in the face of incontrovertible evidence. To do so would be to admit failure, and that is too painful. Denial seems safer to such people, even though it can have devastating results.

Holly was in grade school when she began wetting herself in class with embarrassing regularity. At the same time, she was also stealing in school, in stores, and in church. Holly's mother, who fielded most of the calls from the teacher and other concerned adults, was committed to getting help for her daughter. But Holly's father resisted. His typical response was "She'll grow out of it." He was also convinced that if Holly was disciplined severely enough, she would stop both behaviors. He persisted in that conviction, despite her lack of progress.

The underlying reason for such denial is shame. If we believe that living the principles of the gospel will result in strong, happy families now and for eternity, family difficulties seem to indicate that something is wrong with us, something that sets us apart from our more successful brothers and sisters. If an unhealthy shame prompts us to hide behind a façade of denial, the problem is compounded. If a healthy shame — a sense of our weakness and need for help — prompts us to seek for solutions, the possibility for healing is opened up.

The true failure, then, lies not in having difficulties but in denying them because of an unhealthy shame. In that case, we not only deny ourselves and our loved ones a chance for progress, we also deny the power of the Atonement, which is the power for change. Seeking help is thus an expression of faith in the sort of creatures we are — children of God — and the sort of creatures we may yet become.

CHAPTER 4

THE FAMILY AS A SYSTEM

What is a family?

On the surface, that seems like an easy question to answer, and I suspect that most of us could give a rational definition. However, our understanding of how a family *functions* is based on feeling rather than logic. It is more subconscious than conscious. Most people don't really know what drives their family as a unit. In fact, focus on the family as a unit or a system is a comparatively recent development.

Prior to the '50s, an individual experiencing difficulties was treated as if his problems existed in isolation. Therapy focused solely on the disturbed child, the suicidal teen, the depressed mother, or the addicted husband. The role of the family itself was rarely called into question.

That began to change when psychologists started to consider the environment of their clients. Alfred Adler was one of the first in the field to believe that a person could not be helped unless he was understood in the context of the family and the society in which he lived. Adler studied children in their homes and schools, as well as in the family education centers that he set up. He emphasized the family group, thus indirectly contributing to the development of family-systems theories.

Probably the most important of these theories is that a family cannot be understood as a simple mathematical equation: father + mother + child + child = family. Rather, the family is best understood in terms of physics.

Let's say, for example, that individual family members are represented as electrical transformers. Their relationship is represented by a power line stretching between each and every other family member. Father and mother form the first connection. When a child is born, two more lines are drawn, one representing the relationship between child and mother and one representing that between child and father. The advent of a second child would create three more connections: child 2 — mother, child 2 — father, and child 2 — child 1. The more children in the family, the more lines.

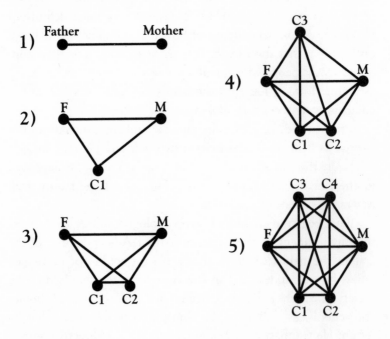

This system of transformers and power lines can be thought

of as an energy grid. The interaction between family members would be the energy constantly moving along the power lines. Each connection or relationship has its own particular level and kind of energy, which affects the energy pattern of the grid as a whole. Perhaps a father and a son have a poor relationship. When conflict sends a surge of negative energy (anger, for example) between them, it also sets in motion a particular pattern of energy flow (reactions, in this case) throughout the entire grid, which affects all family members.

Taking the analogy further, if you were to look at a plan that indicated the placement of several transformers (family members) and the connecting lines (relationships), it wouldn't tell you much. A more useful plan would indicate both the level of energy passing between specific pairs and typical patterns of energy flow throughout the system as a whole. Interaction — the pattern of energy flow between family members — is thus the real defining element of a family.

Survival, the Prime Function

Once a system (whether a family, an organization, or a government) is in place, its prime function becomes survival. If something threatens its survival, members of the system react in a way that will restore balance. In a family system, individuals take on particular roles to keep that balance. They usually do so without being consciously aware of what they are doing or why. The following story illustrates a family system dependent for survival upon having a scapegoat, that is, someone upon whom the dissatisfaction of other family members can be focused.

The Joneses weren't getting along well. Mike was angry and upset at his wife about a long list of things. Pam had a list of grievances toward her husband that was just as long. However, neither one of them talked openly with the other about their grievances, for they didn't feel comfortable about facing their issues directly.

They didn't have time to anyway because their daughter Cindra was causing them a lot of trouble. They spent much of their time every day dealing with Cindra, worrying about her, talking to each other, teachers, and friends about her problems. Their unhappiness with each other was redirected toward this child, whom they felt was the primary source of difficulties in their marriage.

Neither Mike nor Pam had any clue as to the real dynamics of their family situation. In an effort to help Cindra, they took her to a therapist, hoping the therapist could straighten her out. The therapist listened to their story, then suggested that the problem was as much theirs as Cindra's.

They were outraged. They saw no connection between their child's behavior and their relationship. Their relationship wasn't perfect, but it wasn't all that bad!

In the next few sessions, the therapist showed how Cindra was the scapegoat for the Jones family. Her function was to preserve her parents' marriage and thus the family unit. How did she do that? By developing a range of behavioral difficulties that kept her parents focused on her rather than each other. When united by the common goal of dealing with her, they didn't have to deal directly with their own troubled relationship. All the anger and frustration they felt toward each other could be directed toward their problem child.

Luckily for Cindra, the therapist was able to help her understand what was going on. She learned how to separate herself from the family situation, to make decisions based on her own needs, and to take care of herself. This was difficult, since she was still living at home, but she managed.

To the surprise of everyone in the family, as Cindra got better, her little sister seemed to get worse. In fact, she was soon as troubled as Cindra had been. Only the therapist wasn't surprised. She realized that the system the family had established demanded that someone be "the problem" so that an individual rather than the underlying issues would be the focus. When Cindra stopped playing that role, her sister took it over.

You might be asking why anyone would willfully avoid discovering and working on the real issues behind a family's difficulties. In many cases, the avoidance isn't conscious. Those involved honestly do not realize that the person who seems to be the problem is responding to deeper, unresolved issues. They think they are doing what they should in focusing on that individual. In other cases, the avoidance is conscious, based on a fear that articulating the deeper issues will only be "stirring up a can of worms," with disastrous results.

Either way, unresolved issues force individuals into assuming certain roles for the benefit of the family system. Scapegoat is only one example. Other common roles are Hero, Little Mother, and Peacemaker. The Hero is a family member who is idolized or constantly praised to the neglect of others. This focus on the Hero and his accomplishments allows the family to shift attention away from issues that are causing problems. The Little Mother role is taken on by a daughter when the actual mother in the family is not able to fill her function due to illness, psychological problems, addiction, or death. The daughter steps into the void left by mother's absence, taking on much of the burden that rightly belongs to an adult. The Peacemaker, often the third child, tries to defuse conflict whenever it appears, even when the peacemaking is done at his or her expense.

As individuals play out these or other assigned roles, they perpetuate the underlying unhealthy pattern of the family. Ironically, the harder they work to make things better, the more immobilized the family becomes.

When a family member decides to stop playing the assigned

29

role, the system is thrown off balance. This is exactly what is needed, though, because it provides a chance for everyone to relate to each other in different ways. However, other family members typically feel as though that individual is embarking on a destructive course. They can't imagine the family relating in any other way, so they feel that the survival of the family is being threatened. Actually, what is threatened is the survival of the *system*. The family, if all members are willing, can create a new and healthier system. In most cases, however, the family puts a great deal of pressure on all members to maintain their roles.

Family Systems Are Complex

The reason families can get caught in negative systems of behavior is that the rules and roles governing family behavior are passed down primarily on a subconscious level. We often do not know why we react the way we do. In quieter moments, we may make a resolution that we won't react that way again — but within days or even hours, we're right back where we were before.

Why? Vincent Foley explained it this way, "Family systems are powerful precisely because they 'hook' an individual in his 'guts' more than in his head."[1] Logic and will-power don't have much to do with family patterns.

In spite of this, people rarely take the time and effort to learn about the dynamics of family living, unless their family is in turmoil. That is dangerous, says Virginia Satir, author of *Peoplemaking*. She writes:

> Family life is something like an iceberg. Most people are aware of only about one-tenth of what is actually going on — the tenth that they can see and hear — and often they think that is all there is. Some suspect that there may be more, but they don't know what it is and have no idea how to find out. Not knowing can set the family on a dangerous

30

course. Just as a sailor's fate depends on knowing about the iceberg *under* the water, so a family's fate depends on understanding the feelings and needs and patterns that lie beneath everyday things.[2]

If it is irresponsible to remain in ignorance of the behavior patterns upon which our daily habits of interaction are built, how do we begin discovering them? As a first step, you may wish to answer the questions in each of the categories listed below. Your answers will provide insight into how your family works and the areas where change may be appropriate.

Communication: What can be said and what can't? Are needs and wants directly communicated?

Family rules: What are the family rules concerning money? Punishment? Having fun? Achievement?

Family roles: Who is the peacemaker? Who is the clown? Who is the boss? The caretaker?

Family network (this is the grid of power lines discussed earlier): How do different pairs of family members interact with each other?

Family system—open or closed (this has to do with the availability of information from outside the family): Is new information about issues such as relationships, money, or sex welcome?

For those who wish more information on family patterns, I have listed several sources in the References section of this book.

CHAPTER 5

THE PARAMETERS OF DYSFUNCTION

A further understanding of how families operate as systems has come from the work done with alcoholics and other substance abusers and their families. We have come to recognize that an abuser is not the only one with a problem: the entire family has a problem.

Family members, therapists realize, react in an unhealthy way to the stress placed on them by the abuser. They may act as a buffer between the abuser and the consequences of his actions. They may make excuses to his superiors, to other family members, and to friends. They will usually do whatever is necessary to maintain a semblance of normal family life, while at the same time guarding the family against the disaster that threatens them.

Therapists use the term *codependents* to describe the family members caught up in this unhealthy pattern. They use the term *codependency* to describe attitudes and behaviors characteristic of these family members.

Codependents have generally become obsessed with other people. They have turned outward so much that, instead of managing and living their own lives, they pour their energies into managing and living other peoples' lives. They may focus on one particular person, on their entire family, or even on a broader group.

Control is an issue for codependents. One woman made a statement that illustrates this perfectly: "I can't stand the fact that I can't make the universe turn for my girls." She says she can't control the people and events that affect her children's lives, yet she still tries to—and gets frustrated and angry when she fails.

Codependents make great employees, for they work hard at doing the right thing. They are very concerned with their image, and they put considerable energy into pleasing people. Managers can get a lot of extra work out of codependents by playing on their need for approval and on their overdeveloped sense of responsibility.

Numerous therapists have identified many of the character-istics typical of codependents.[1] I have included some of them here. Codependents may

- focus their energies on others
- be obsessed with every aspect of others' lives, no matter how minor
- try to change others to fit their expectations
- become inordinately upset when events do not progress the way they want them to, even when they are not responsible for the outcome
- attempt to control events and people by manipulating; guilting; assuming responsibility; threatening; withholding love, support, or information; acting helpless, or becoming ill (yet feel they are at the mercy of people and events)
- not be able to communicate their own needs clearly
- be disappointed or angry when others do not respond to their unexpressed needs
- take on others' emotions, like anger, sorrow, or disap-pointment, and express them as their own

33

- take responsibility for others' problems and attempt to solve them
- base their self-worth on externals
- be devastated when others react to them negatively
- fear making mistakes or looking foolish, so avoid taking risks

Once information about codependency began appearing in popular self-help literature, an interesting phenomenon occurred. People who were seeking help because of issues unrelated to substance abuse saw themselves mirrored in the books they were reading. Victims of physical or sexual abuse saw their own feelings described. Persons responsible for the care of the elderly and terminally ill suddenly felt less alone. Parents and siblings whose lives revolved around a severely handicapped child realized they were not wicked or selfish for having negative thoughts. Women and men whose spouses were rigid and controlling heaved sighs of recognition. Many were relieved to discover that what they were experiencing had a name and that help was available to them.

As a result of the feedback that professionals got from such people, they realized that a broader range of circumstances resulted in dysfunctional relationships than had been previously thought. Charles Whitfield wrote, for example, "Families of alcoholism; physical, emotional, or sexual abuse; mental or physical illness; perfectionism and rigidity; or codependence can fit into the dysfunctional spectrum, depending on the severity."[2] The categories listed in this statement cover an incredibly broad range. Based on this wider view, family therapists have come to the following conclusions:

Every family is dysfunctional to some degree. While that statement may seem obvious, many perpetuate the myth of perfect families by denying their problems and maintaining their public

34

image. In doing so, they encourage unrealistic expectations in their children, who are often poorly equipped to deal with the realities of marriage and family life. They are greatly relieved when they discover what Earnie Larson states so succinctly: "There are no perfect people; there are no perfect family systems."[3]

A dysfunctional family doesn't offer needed emotional support. A family may provide for the physical needs of its members and yet be unable to provide those things needed for growth and prosperity: love, acceptance, communication, support, encouragement, and autonomy. In severely dysfunctional families, this is always the case. In families with less severe problems, the lack of emotional support occurs primarily when circumstances are stressful.

Dysfunction leads to compulsive or addictive behavior. When individual growth is not supported or encouraged in a family, its members often turn to compulsive behaviors and addictions as a way of dealing with the pain.

Denial creates more dysfunction. Accepting the fact that a problem exists is the first step toward solving it. Denying that a problem exists not only leaves the initial problem unsolved, it also adds to an already unhealthy situation. John Bradshaw says, "The difference between a functional family and a dysfunctional family is that a functional family will solve its problems. A dysfunctional family will deny the problems and act as if the problems don't exist or will try to create roles that keep the problems frozen in the center of their lives."[4]

Dysfunction is a social issue. Families reflect the society in which they live. If many families are dysfunctional to some degree, then something in our society contributes to that dysfunction. According to experts, our schools and churches encourage us to think and feel the way authority figures tell us we should think and feel. When we abdicate our right to choose for ourselves,

35

we put ourselves at risk for developing addictive and codependent behaviors.

Dysfunction is a spiritual issue. Finally, dysfunction is a block to both emotional and spiritual growth. It cuts us off from ourselves, from those around us, and from God. Thus, the issues we address when dealing with dysfunction are ultimately spiritual issues. If we are committed to the gospel and to spiritual growth, we must have the courage to face these issues and find ways to deal with them appropriately.

CHAPTER 6

REPRESSIVE RULES

In the first chapter two questions were raised: What went wrong? and, How can we make it right? In this chapter we will begin to look at some current ideas about what went wrong. They may come as a surprise, because many of us don't look for underlying causes when attempting to solve family problems. We focus on the irritation of the moment. An often-used analogy describes perfectly what we do: we put a bandage on what we think is a surface wound, not realizing that the whole body is suffering from a systemic disease.

The difficulties that many families in our society are experiencing result from the rules that we have used in rearing children. Although there have been numerous enlightened books and classes on child-rearing in recent decades, most of us were reared — and are rearing our children — according to rules dating back to the times when children were property of the head of the household and the father legally held all of the power and all of the rights.

Even though the legal system has instituted many changes leading to a more equitable distribution of rights and power in family units, many of the attitudes and beliefs springing from

37

this time are still in evidence. They have been perpetuated in part by the Judeo-Christian tradition, which holds that the husband is the head of the household in the same manner that Christ is the head of the church. This would not be problematic but for the fact that power is so often misused. Doctrine and Covenants 121:39 contains the statement "It is the nature and disposition of almost all men, as soon as they get a little authority, . . . they will immediately begin to exercise unrighteous dominion."[1]

Members may not think of this scripture in terms of parenting. They may not realize the destructive nature of the controlling, domineering manner in which they relate to family members. They may think that they are doing what they are supposed to be doing, that is, training up their children in the way they should go. Feeling the heavy burden of parenthood, they may believe that they are justified in using whatever means necessary to teach their child to conform to the expectations of both the larger society and their particular subgroup, in this case, the Mormon culture.

In general, adults parent the way they were parented. Unfortunately, many of the parenting patterns passed on from generation to generation reflect the older, autocratic methods of parenting, much of which is repressive. These repressive parenting patterns stifle the openness, trust, and ability to love that is present in every child, resulting in dysfunction. No wonder that Alice Miller refers to repressive parenting as "poisonous pedagogy."[1]

"Poisonous pedagogy" involves a set of negative beliefs about relationships and behavior. Children reared repressively assimilate these beliefs, accepting them as valid. Unless they challenge them as adults, the beliefs learned in childhood will form the basis for their actions — conscious or unconscious — throughout

38

their lives. In her book *For Your Own Good,* Alice Miller enumerates eleven such false beliefs:

1. A feeling of duty produces love.
2. Hatred can be done away with by forbidding it.
3. Parents deserve respect because they are parents.
4. Obedience makes a child strong.
5. A high degree of self-esteem is harmful.
6. A pretense of gratitude is better than honest ingratitude.
7. The way you behave is more important than the way you really are.
8. Neither parents nor God would survive being offended.
9. Strong feelings are harmful.
10. Parents are creatures free of drive and guilt.
11. Parents are always right.[2]

Most of us have a limited awareness of how these beliefs inform our parenting because they were transmitted to us more or less indirectly. We carry them in nonverbal forms in our subconscious. They become activated in moments of stress, with the result that we do and say the very things we promised ourselves we as parents would never do or say!

Following are examples of typical parental statements, each of which relates to one of the beliefs stated above. To those of us who grew up hearing similar statements from our parents and other adults, they seem so commonplace that we may be shocked to realize the messages they convey to our children.

1. A Feeling of Duty Produces Love

"If you do it long enough, you'll get to like it."

We are often taught that if we do what we should, which in this situation is usually what others expect of us, everything will turn out for the best, whether it's taking piano lessons, eating

39

broccoli, or going on a mission. This notion would convince us that we can act in opposition to our thoughts and feelings with the result that our thoughts and feelings will change. This is not usually so, except in cases where there is a desire for a changed attitude. The risk in such an approach is that it can make us feel increasingly angry, resentful, rebellious, with increasingly negative results.

This example also draws upon rule seven, which states that behavior is more important than what the individual really thinks and feels. We sense that who we really are and what we really need aren't important. This leads us to doubt ourselves and encourages us to create a false self that complies with desired behavior.

"Do your chores! Your mother's given you a lot, and it's time you showed her you love her."

All parents want to know that their children love them. In healthy families, that love is frequently expressed in seemingly insignificant, routine ways. In a family where parents are stern and authoritarian, children may not feel particularly loving or grateful. Doing their duty — taking care of chores — may be needful, but it won't create affection if it is missing.

2. Hatred Can Be Done Away with by Forbidding It

"Don't say you hate your little brother. I know you don't really feel that way."

Though we realize that hate itself can be damaging, the danger in this belief is the stifling of strong emotions. The powerful parent, who believes that strong emotions are harmful (belief nine) and that they can be done away with by simply forbidding them, negates the child's actual emotions. It is a subtle way of belittling emotion, as though the child's feelings are not legitimate. That parent also probably stifles his or her own strong emotions in an attempt to do away with them.

Emotions that have been dammed up exert considerable force, often erupting in misdirected rage. An example of misdirected rage is the mother who yells at her child for leaving his shoes on the floor, when what really upsets her is the chronic lack of communication between her and her husband. However, she doesn't feel that she can express any of her feelings — disappointment, sorrow, frustration, or anger — to her husband, so she tries to squelch them. Eventually, however, the pressure of these stuffed emotions becomes critical, and she again flies into a rage over something entirely unrelated.

3. Parents Deserve Respect Because They Are Parents

"I want to see some respect from you, young man, or you can spend the rest of the evening in your room."

Every one of us was taught that we should respect our elders, particularly our parents, teachers, and others in authority over us. We were taught to address them politely and to do what they asked us to do. We probably did all of these things, though in some cases with reservation or confusion, for not all adults treat children in a manner deserving of respect. Such a belief assumes that authority is independent of accountability. As parents, we would never teach our children that they are not accountable for their actions, yet we ourselves may be separating our actions as parents from their consequences by demanding respect "no matter what."

This belief is especially detrimental when abuse is involved. One teen was emotionally mistreated for years by her mother. She felt no love and offered no respect for the woman. Her father, who had witnessed her mother's behavior on many occasions, still took her mother's side, demanding that the daughter show some respect, saying, "Your mother's a good woman." It was as though the father was saying that the abuse had never

41

taken place at all, leaving the young woman feeling as though she was losing her mind.

4. Obedience Makes a Child Strong

"There'll always be someone you have to obey: parents, teachers, adults in general, your boss, the law, church authorities, God. It's a hard lesson, but if you learn now to do what you're told, life will be easier for you."

I'm sure we have all experienced a time when we were told we had to do something, regardless of our reasons for not wanting to. Perhaps we were told, "It's for your own good," and maybe it actually was. Many times parental instructions are given for the safety and well-being of their children. But many times they are also given for the comfort, convenience, well-being, and self-esteem of the parent. Children can frequently sense when that is the case.

I remember hearing about a father who told his young child that he had to learn to obey without question because that was how he would learn to obey his Father in Heaven. Not surprisingly, that same father often asked the child to do things that were inappropriate or very difficult for his age or strength in an attempt to teach obedience. He also made arbitrary decisions about what he would allow his teenagers to do, often denying their requests for no good reason. He justified himself by saying things like "God doesn't always let us do what we want to do. I'm just treating my children the way God treats his children."

We parents (and other adults) are too fallible to require absolute obedience in all things from our children. Besides which, doing so robs them of the freedom to make their own choices as appropriate to their age and development.

Also, obedience for its own sake is not a virtue. When children are brought up in homes requiring strict and immediate obedience, they learn that obedience is the greatest good. They learn to disregard their own thoughts and feelings, which in turn thwarts the development of their conscience. In addition, since they are often not given the opportunity to make decisions on their own, even when appropriate, their ability to do so is seriously stunted. Requiring strict obedience can even be a rather brutal attempt to destroy all that is individualistic about a person.

5. A High Degree of Self-esteem Is Harmful

"Don't get too cocky. 'Pride goeth before a fall.' "

Self-absorption and inordinate focus on personal accomplishments do harm relationships. That is not the issue here, however. In this case, parents can sabotage the confidence, self-esteem, and enthusiasm of their children by such statements.

Sometimes that is exactly the parents' goal. They may honestly think that being too confident is not good for children, for fear that the children will get hurt or fail. Or they may think that it is not in line with the humility spoken of in the scriptures. Or they may fear that it will prompt the children to follow their own vision, rather than do what the family or community expects them to do. Parents who have lived their lives according to others' expectations tend to feel uncomfortable, even angry, if their children do not feel bound to do well in those areas their parents think are important.

6. A Pretense of Gratitude Is Better
Than Honest Ingratitude

"I don't care if you don't like that sweater. You go give Auntie Ellen a kiss and tell her you love it."

Even though the intent of this rule is positive — not to hurt another — such a request puts children in a quandary, for they are asked to tell a lie. While the concept of "white lies" may make some sense to older children and adults, it doesn't to younger children. Although they wouldn't express their feeling

43

in exactly those terms, they sense that they have been asked to compromise their integrity, to be hypocritical.

This rule also incorporates some of rule seven, which states that what you do is more important than what you are. It creates a gap between the inner and outer self, and the child will end up either lying or repressing his or her real feelings to please the parent, or choosing to go against the parental injunction, which puts one in an awkward position.

7. The Way You Behave Is More Important Than the Way You Really Are

"You may be depressed, but nobody likes a sourpuss. Go to your room until you can come out with a smile on your face."

As with other parental statements based on repressive rules, these words contain some truth. Consciously choosing to present a cheerful demeanor despite negative feelings can be helpful, if the person also acknowledges his true feelings and resolves the issues relating to them. This requires skills and knowledge that children don't have. Unless the parent helps them with the process, the lesson they may learn from such statements is that their false self is more acceptable than their authentic self.

Many parents motivated even subconsciously by rule seven try to control all aspects of their children's lives, including the way they dress, the grades they get, the friends they choose, the hobbies they have, and the career they pursue. In such cases, the parents are more interested in seeing their children conform to the mental image they have of children than letting them express themselves openly and develop their unique gifts.

8. Neither Parents Nor God Would Survive Being Offended

"Don't you dare say how you feel to your mother! She would never get over it!"

Such words would lead us to believe that knowing the truth about what is happening in our personal relationships can be dangerous, even fatal. They also reflect rule nine, which states that strong feelings are harmful. In addition, some interpret rule three in such a way that they feel disagreeing with parents would be disrespectful, even when disagreeing would be telling the truth. Such people do not realize that disagreement normally has nothing to do with disrespect or respect. In an argument, however, a person's emotions may lead them to make an illogical link between the two.

9. Strong Feelings Are Harmful

"Don't get carried away with your feelings. Calm down and think rationally about it."

Of course there are times, such as in the heat of an argument, when calmness is greatly needed. But negative feelings are not an issue here. Rule nine is aimed at squelching the strong feelings that result from a healthy involvement in life.

For example, the phrase "calm down" is often used when a child (or adult for that matter) is excited about something out of the ordinary, something that doesn't fit parental or spousal expectations, something that may be risky. The intent is to rob the individual of the energy propelling him toward this unwelcome expression of individuality.

I remember the gleam in our oldest daughter's eyes when she excitedly returned to our temporary home in Erkrath, Germany, to announce that she had figured out how to stay another year after the rest of us returned to Minnesota. She was so full of plans, so confident in her ability to take care of herself during this time!

Gary and I, on the other hand, could think of a hundred reasons why returning to Minnesota and attending Macalester College as planned would be better for her. In less than ten minutes, we managed to wipe the smile off her face and dampen the gleam in her eye. After many stormy discussions, we finally realized that she had a viable plan and that delaying her studies another year wouldn't be a tragedy. Too bad we weren't able to let go of our expectations — and fears — long enough to enjoy her excitement in the newfound possibilities.

10. Parents Are Creatures Free of Drives and Guilt

"You never see me or your father doing that sort of thing! You'd better get your life under control."

A funny thing happens to some people when they become parents: They forget all the silly, dangerous things they ever did. They forget the intense feelings that prompted certain decisions. They forget their mistakes and failures. They no longer admit they are human. They put themselves up as examples for their children — but they don't hold up their authentic selves for show, they tout their false selves. Children who grow up in such homes can develop false selves as well.

Parents who are willing to reveal themselves to their children give them a great gift. They give them examples of what it's like to be human, to hurt, to strive, to triumph, to grieve, to err, to laugh, to love, and even to be outrageous now and then. They give them the freedom to be themselves and to express their uniqueness. How wonderful such a legacy is!

11. Parents Are Always Right

"Don't question what I'm saying. I know what's best for you."

This belief is a clear expression of the notion "Might makes right." In other words, the one who has the power is the one who has all the answers. It is the key to all of the other ten beliefs and the parental behaviors arising from them. When children are rendered powerless by autocratic parents, they learn only how to become autocratic parents themselves. When they become parents, they treat their children as they were treated, which in an odd way allows them to recover their lost power — at the expense of their children's well-being. When we consider that children often cope with abuse by believing that their parent's actions are justified because they deserve to be punished, we can easily see how those same children can grow up feeling justified in their own abusive behaviors — emotional, verbal, physical, or sexual — toward the next generation.

I recently encountered a humorous example of "doing away with hatred by forbidding it." A preschooler screamed "I hate you" at his mother. The mother sharply responded, "You don't." The conversation quickly escalated to an ear-piercing "Yes I do," "No you don't," "Do," "Don't." I doubt that the mother convinced the child that he didn't know his own feelings. But if she tells him so often enough, he could eventually come to believe that she knows his feelings better than he does. Then, when he does have strong feelings about something, he will be ashamed.

In June of 1989, I had a more serious encounter with "poisonous pedagogy." I participated in a week-long ecology camp in the Bohemian forest of Czechoslovakia. Part of the entertainment that week was provided by the Priessental Theater group, a traveling troup from West Germany. The play they presented was entitled *Ratcatcher*. Since the ratcatcher in the original legend is called the pied piper in the English translation, I took my seat expecting to see an enjoyable retelling of *The Pied Piper of Hamelin*. And indeed, that was the way the play began.

The tone changed very quickly, however. The ratcatcher, the one who lured away a whole generation of children, was not a man piping a merry tune. According to the new presentation, which was written by troupe members, the generation of German children born after World War I were led into pain, sorrow, and violence by their own parents — or more precisely, by the re-

47

pressive rules the parents used in rearing them, and which they in turn used to rear their own children. The Ratcatcher, in this case, was "poisonous pedagogy" itself. In comical but more often painful scenes, the effects of what the troupe called "black pedagogy" were shown beginning in the years directly after World War I and continuing through World War II.

The play was an indictment of the societal rules governing Germany during those decades. But larger implications were unavoidable. While the scenes were set in a different time and place, many of them were poignant because the patterns and beliefs were sadly familiar. *Ratcatcher* was a voice of warning to all. Violence is done to children when they are neither allowed to live their own lives, nor to experience and think about what they see and hear, when authority invalidates their experiences. Unwavering adherence to parental expectations and unthinking obedience to those in authority are seeds of destruction, regardless of where or by whom they are planted.

CHAPTER 7

SHAME: THE MASTER EMOTION

The goal of repressive rules is to control children — to make them do what they're supposed to do and to feel what they're supposed to feel. No doubt you have witnessed scenes in which a child at play is told, "Stop being so noisy," or "Stop running around so much." As a society, we like our children best when they're quiet and careful rather than boisterous and energetic. We like them best when they do what they're told without questioning the validity of it. We like them best when they wait for instructions and then follow them.

You may have heard the story of a little girl who learned this lesson very early. She went enthusiastically to kindergarten the first day of school. Her teacher passed out paper and crayons, announcing that they were going to draw flowers. "Good!" thought the little girl. She picked out her favorite colors and began to draw.

The teacher was at her side in an instant. "No, no! Put your crayons down and wait for me to tell you what to do," she said. Then to the whole class she gave instructions. They were to draw a tulip. It was to look like the example she drew on the board. The flower was to be colored red, the stem green. The little girl turned her paper over and did as she was told.

49

Some time later, her family moved to a new house, and she began to attend a different school. One day, the teacher announced that they were going to draw flowers. She passed out paper, and the children took out their crayons. Everyone else began to draw, but the little girl waited quietly for instructions.

"Why aren't you drawing?" asked the teacher.

"You haven't told me what I am supposed to draw yet," she answered.

"You can draw any kind of flower you want. Use your imagination. It's all up to you."

The little girl sat for a long time. Then she picked up her crayons and drew a red tulip with a green stem.

Repressive Rules Lead to Shame

In order to create of our children the socially acceptable persons we want them to be, we all too often discount, make fun of, or completely reject the validity of their thoughts and feelings. As a result, children often learn that expressing what they feel inside isn't safe. They learn to react with shame at their true feelings and thoughts, their impulses, even their basic needs. Because shame is painful, they repress their thoughts, feelings, and needs as a way of avoiding both the shame and the pain. They can get so good at this that they can squelch an impulse almost instantaneously. They can thus be unaware of what is going on inside. They don't understand why they are buffeted by bouts of depression or feelings of anger or futility.

We also need to realize that children can feel shamed, rejected, and unloved not only because of an event, but also because of *what they perceived that event to mean*. The parents and child may remember it quite differently, so the event itself can be less important than the way the child feels about it. Because of this, some situations regarded by the parents as being relatively unimportant can have lasting effects on a child's outlook.

50

Interaction in a healthy family encourages its members to grow. Interaction fosters emotional intimacy but at the same time allows autonomy. Repressive parenting rules are in direct opposition to healthy family interaction. How can emotional intimacy be fostered, for example, if children are not allowed to freely express themselves? How can autonomy be encouraged if the parent is always right?

The False Self

When children learn to feel shame at their own needs, wants, thoughts, and emotions, they can feel powerless and defenseless. All people have a need to protect themselves. To do so, they may repress feelings and create a "false self." This false self is the embodiment of what they think they must be in order to please both others and God.

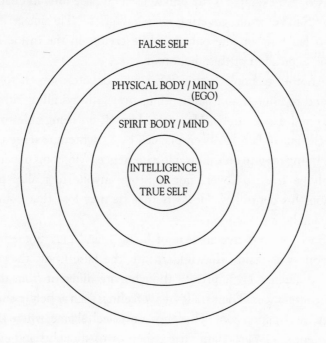

As a result, they refer constantly to sources outside themselves to evaluate their worth and acceptability. Instead of going inside themselves to experience feelings of being OK, they constantly monitor what others think of them. Instead of expressing their feelings and thoughts about an issue, they listen to others until they know what the accepted position is, then they echo it. Their self-esteem rises and falls with the opinion of others. Feelings of self-worth, on the other hand, rise from deeper within, from a person's innate intelligence and spirit body and mind. Self-worth is not subject to what other people think or tell us.

People who are protecting themselves with false selves project an image — one that coincides with the expectations of the society to which they belong. That image is not a reflection of what they feel inside. There is, in fact, often a startling dichotomy between the two. An example is the phrase used on page nine in chapter one, "Sunday smile covering everyday grief." The image of a clown laughing on the outside while crying on the inside is a classic expression of that dichotomy.

Another example is the father who devotes himself to his job and to church and family obligations, always filling others' needs and expectations. He prides himself on being able to do so well, but of late has been plagued by a frightening sense that he is losing his grip on things. He experiences symptoms of panic, which he tries to cover, not wanting anyone to realize how tenuous his control is. He fears that he may lose that control completely one day soon.

Such persons live in fear of being found out. Sometime, someone will realize that underneath the false front, they are quite different. Their private thoughts are different from their public utterances. Their smiles mask feelings such as helplessness, anger, and depression. They not only feel shame when they experience "inappropriate" (i.e., their own) thoughts and emo-

52

tions, but they also feel shame because they know they are living a lie.

The false self is created as a means of protection and survival, but it keeps ourselves and others from knowing who we really are. When we act from the false self, we are being untrue to our nature, which is a form of hypocrisy. We are less open to the promptings of the Holy Spirit. Our spiritual growth is blocked.

Sometimes people identify themselves so closely with the false self that they aren't aware that it is false until some additional stress causes cracks in the facade. One young mother of a large family did everything she thought was expected of young mothers of large families in Utah. She baked, she sewed, she gardened, she read to her children, she said prayers with them before bed, she was active in the Church. She had learned, and she practiced, complete self-reliance.

In spite of the busyness of her life, she was comfortable in her role as mother and felt confident and competent — except for the times she had strange feelings of dis-ease or impending doom. Several times she had mentioned these moments to others, including her physician, who passed them off as normal for a woman in her circumstances.

Then, while in the middle of giving a lesson on the Atonement, the crack appeared. She stopped midsentence as the thought came to her mind that the Atonement was a wonderful thing . . . but it didn't apply to her. At the time, she couldn't quite identify why. Then she realized that she wasn't sure she believed in the Atonement at all! Her shame at teaching a principle that she didn't believe in — and receiving praise for it — led her to ask to be released. Her release compounded the shame further, and her life seemed to unravel, leading to withdrawal and inactivity.

In the darkness of the time that followed, she learned that what had started out as a vague sense of dis-ease had its roots in repressed memories of childhood violence and abuse. As the memories emerged, she discovered that inside the woman who baked bread and sewed and gardened and said prayers with her children at night was "a whole other self who had lived a whole other life."

Shame: The Master Emotion

Shame has been referred to in recent literature as the "master emotion." The kind of shame professionals are referring to in this case is not what might be considered normal, healthy shame at the recognition of our human weaknesses. It is a destructive emotion that leads to an all-pervasive sense of being flawed and defective as a human being.

There is a significant difference between guilt and this kind of shame. I like the way Charles Whitfield explains it:[1] "Guilt is the uncomfortable or painful feeling that results from doing something that violates or breaks a personal standard or value. . . . Guilt thus concerns our *behavior*. [It] can be a useful emotion to help guide us in our relationships with ourselves and others. Guilt tells us our consciousness is functioning. Guilt can be relieved substantially by recognizing its presence and then *working it through*."

People experiencing unhealthy shame have no sense that there is any solution available to them. The shame they feel is the central fact of their lives, often since childhood. It has seriously impaired their capacity to express the spontaneously loving, curious, creative, exuberant, happy, outgoing, risk-taking selves they were as children. The dynamics of this sad development may be illustrated in the following examples:

Sarah falls and skins her knee. Experiencing pain, she comes crying to her mother, who says, "Stop blubbering! You're not hurt that bad." She learns from the experience and countless others like it to feel ashamed at expressing emotion.

54

Billy is curious about everything! He loves to explore, and he loves to take things apart. In his eyes, the world is a giant playground, full of wonderful things for him to discover. But his father gets impatient when he asks questions or takes things apart and then needs help in reassembling them. He is often told, "Stop making a mess! Go to your room, read a book, and stay out of trouble!" After hearing this many times, Billy becomes ashamed whenever he has the desire to explore or question.

Max is always trying something new. He loves the excitement of forging into untried territory. A born risk-taker, he fails at his endeavours more often than he succeeds, but that doesn't matter to him. It's the excitement and the learning that he loves — although as a youngster he doesn't think of it in those words. His parents make fun of him. "There you go again," they say, shaking their heads. "Try not to come home with something broken, if that's possible." Or they say something like, "You look silly trying to do those skateboard tricks, especially when you crash. Why don't you do yourself a favor and give it up." Eventually, Max learns to be ashamed of his risk-taking approach to life.

Marsha is a Pollyanna. She is pleased with everything life has to offer. Her attitude angers her grandmother who says bitterly, "Go ahead. Walk around with that silly grin on your face. But enjoy it while you can. Life isn't all that rosy. It'll get you sooner or later." Marsha begins to feel that her love of life is based on naïveté and is ashamed that she doesn't see the serious, dangerous aspects.

Because of the adult reactions to their natural love of life, these children each learn to feel ashamed. The shame is so closely associated with their emotions, needs, and thoughts that every time they experience any of them, they also inevitably experience the shame as well. They have become shame-based.

This phenomenon has led professionals to refer to unhealthy

55

shame as the master emotion. In people who have experienced destructive, repressive parenting, shame becomes tied to every life-affirming expression of their real self. To compound the problem, when the pain of shame becomes intolerable, such individuals often turn to some compulsive or addictive behavior that results in a fleeting feeling of wholeness. The aftermath, however, is increased shame and self-hatred, which fuels the cycle.

Because unhealthy shame profoundly affects our behavior, it is important that we learn to honor our feelings, wants, and needs rather than be ashamed of them. This may be a lengthy process, but the more we discover and honor them, the more we become aware of our authentic selves. And when we act from our authentic selves, we discover a new enthusiasm for life and a powerful energy that can be directed toward developing positive coping techniques.

CHAPTER 8

THE ROLE OF STRESS

The third common denominator in dysfunctional families is some behavior, attitude, or event that puts particular stress on the family unit. I will refer to these as stressors.

Problems, whether they result from choices or chance, put stress on a family. The family's response will minimize or exacerbate the stress. The healthier family is more likely to adapt to stressful circumstances in ways not harmful. The needs of individual family members for validation, emotional intimacy, and growth will still be met with reasonable consistency.

However, even a healthy family can become dysfunctional if their response to stressful circumstances is such that it stops meeting the emotional and growth needs of individuals. For example, let's say a husband has lost his job. He feels like a failure. In fact, he feels extreme shame. The shame is too painful to acknowledge, so he covers it with anger. The wife tells the children that they must not talk to anyone about what is happening, not even to their father. They must act as if everything is normal. This injunction adds yet more stress, and the children become tense. They are constantly on guard, fearing they will reveal the family secret or do something to elicit their father's rage.

This response to stress may be only temporary, especially if the stress is temporary. Suppose the husband finds a job within a few weeks that can pay the bills. He feels as if an immense burden is lifted from him, for he no longer carries the shame of being a man who can't provide for his family. As his anger dissipates, the tension his wife and children felt lessens. Now that they don't have to tip-toe around the ogre anymore, they begin to laugh and play again. Family life returns to normal patterns of behavior.

In some cases, getting back to normal is not so easy because the event that caused the stress in the first place is irreversible or the condition that caused it is chronic. Perhaps there has been a death or a divorce or a sudden, permanent loss of employment. Perhaps a severely handicapped child has been born into the family. Perhaps a family member has a compulsive or addictive behavior pattern that is increasing in its intensity. Perhaps a parent suffers from a chronic illness such as severe depression or a progressively debilitating disease such as Parkinson's.

When families react to chronic stress in unhealthy ways, they can create a dysfunctional pattern of relating that, if not altered, is perpetuated by the succeeding generations. The three specific stressors I wish to comment on particularly are 1) the marriage partnership, 2) compulsive, addictive, and codependent behaviors, and 3) perfectionism.

The Marriage Partnership

Often, a troubled marriage is the prime stressor.

In our society, young people do not receive adequate information about how a family unit functions. That is not surprising, given the fact that relatively few adults understand it themselves. As a result, most young people contemplating marriage do not understand very much about the attitudes, behaviors, roles, and rules they learned in their own families. They understand even less about the way those factors operate in their loved one's family, to say nothing of how the two sets of rules, roles, and behaviors in combination are influencing their relationship with each other.

The result is that few young people realize that part of the reason they are attracted to each other may be the fact that the ways of interrelating they learned in their respective families are complementary—they feel comfortable with each other. That is not necessarily a plus for the couple. The woman who learned from her mother that being helpless is a positive feminine trait will seek out, perhaps unawares, a man who learned from his father that being in control is a postive masculine trait. When she finds the man who will tell her what to do and take care of her, she will feel a click, an instant sense of familiarity, which she interprets as love. In my novel *The Broken Covenant,* main character Kathy contemplates what brought her and her husband together. She concludes it was less a matter of love than a matter of compatible neuroses!

A dysfunctional partnership is not necessarily one in which overt conflict is present. Remember the example of Ann, who, following her parents' example, never addressed difficult issues or expressed anger or other negative emotions.

Compulsive, Addictive, and Codependent Behaviors

Compulsive or addictive behaviors are both reactions to stress and stressors. An astonishingly wide range of behaviors fall into this category, including

1. Substance abuse: drugs, alcohol, food (bulimia, anorexia, compulsive overeating).
2. Compulsive behaviors attached to gambling, shopping, pornography.

3. Compulsive behaviors that are abusive: self-injury, physical or sexual abuse of others.
4. Addiction to emotions incident to crisis management or rage (adrenaline), the resolutions of other people's problems (self-righteousness), or religious experiences (euphoria).
5. Addiction to activities used to detract from pain: work, sports, or exercise.
6. Addiction to activities used to numb oneself: TV watching, reading, thinking obsessively, sleeping, feeling ill.

This list is often surprising. It is difficult to accept the idea that basically positive (or even necessary) activities like eating, exercise, and church work can be addictions. I was surprised myself until I read an advice column that included the list of questions prepared by Alcoholics Anonymous as a test for alcoholism. I found that if I substituted the word *food* for *alcohol* and the word *eat* for *drink,* I would have had to answer yes to enough questions to be considered an addict. As if that weren't enough, I had the same addictive patterns in regard to compulsive reading, TV-watching, and shopping. They were all activities I used as a way of avoiding pain.

John Bradshaw says we engage in these activities so that we don't know "how lonely, hurt, mad and sad" we really are. He emphasizes the pervasiveness of the problem when he says, "Addiction has become our national lifestyle (or rather death style)."[1]

A person caught up in compulsive or addictive behavior puts tremendous stress on others in the family. The chronic behavior becomes the central focus of their lives, and they respond to it by developing coping mechanisms. Some typical coping mechanisms are denial, repression of feelings, withdrawal, anger, and addictive behavior. Family members whose lives are focused on

the compulsive or addictive behavior of another are called codependents.

The coping mechanisms typical of codependency give the
family members some sense of control and help them survive at
critical junctures, but they are ultimately destructive. As they
become internalized, they affect every part of the individual's
life, even when the primary stress (the compulsive/addictive behavior of a family member) is not immediate. For example, adults
who grew up in dysfunctional families may still react to people
and events with the negative coping patterns they developed as
children. (For more about codependency, see chapter 11.)

Perfectionism

Codependents are often perfectionists. They are inordinately
concerned more with how things look — with image and results —
than with people and processes. Their sense of worth, of safety,
and of peace are all dependent on whether things meet the
standards they have adopted to please others. Despite the fact
that these people are often difficult to be around, they are valued
by society, because they are the ones who get things done. They
drive themselves and everyone around them toward accomplishment of their goals.

Perfectionists are sometimes so concerned with the image
that when something goes wrong, they can't bear to acknowledge
it. Whatever the problem — financial difficulties, a teenage pregnancy, the homosexuality of a child, the dishonorable release of
a missionary, substance abuse, physical or sexual abuse — it becomes *the secret*. It is the thing everyone in the family is aware
of, but no one talks about. Family members all do their part in
maintaining silence, but at great cost. The issue becomes central
to the family, with all members stuck in certain roles around it.

Not surprisingly, perfectionists don't often make good parents, for their standards of behavior are difficult to measure up

to. However, we should also note that the opposite of rigid, punitive, judgmental parenting can create dysfunction as well. In chaotic families, there are indistinct boundaries and unclear rules. Problems are typically allowed to reach crisis proportions before they are dealt with. Meeting the needs of individuals for emotional satisfaction and growth is certainly not likely in such conditions.

CHAPTER 9

PERFECTIONISM IN LATTER-DAY SAINT SOCIETY

Families do not exist in a vacuum. They are part of larger systems, such as organizations or institutions. Those in turn are encompassed by even larger systems, such as ethnic groups, regions, or nations. Each system has a particular way of seeing things. Smaller systems usually accept many of the values expressed by the larger systems to which they belong. They also often put extra emphasis on a particular value accepted by the whole.

For example, the drive to perfect individuals and society is part of our American culture. It is well-expressed in the words of a French healer that were popularized in America by positive-thinking advocates. I learned them from my mother, who learned them from her mother: "Every day in every way I get better and better." The value of perfecting oneself and society is accepted and enlarged upon in LDS culture by the particular beliefs Latter-day Saints hold about the scripture "Be ye therefore perfect" (Matt. 5:48). Many Latter-day Saints feel a greater need to be perfect than their non-LDS neighbors. Unfortunately, their beliefs are largely based on "member teachings," not the teachings of the Church or the gospel, and the results can be destructive, opposite to those desired.

After the appearance of my novel *The Broken Covenant*, I was often asked why I wrote a book about adultery. The question surprised me because I had not set out to write a book on that theme. To me, the book was about other things, among them the need to take personal responsibility for actions, the destructive results of faulty communication, the power of forgiveness, and the effects of perfectionism. The adultery and its aftermath were plot elements by which those themes were illuminated.

The major theme developed in *The Broken Covenant* was the effects of perfectionism. The theme was introduced in the following quote, which appears at the front of the book, from Viktor Frankl's *Man's Search For Meaning:* "I doubt that they [the saints] ever had it in mind to become saints. If that were the case, they would have become perfectionists."[1]

All Church members are perfectionists, at least according to the first part of Webster's definition: *One who believes in the ethical or spiritual perfectability of mankind.* As Latter-day Saints, we seek for nothing less; the perfecting of the Saints is the stated purpose of the restoration of the gospel.

Too often, however, we become perfectionists of the type described in the second part of Webster's definition: *One who rejects anything short of perfection as unacceptable.* This second definition describes the sort of perfectionism that Viktor Frankl was warning against, for it puts more emphasis on the letter of the law than the spirit, on form rather than content.

We are all caught up in perfectionism to one degree or another. But some who adopt this standard become obsessed by the need to perfect themselves and others around them. They act as if they have forgotten the Atonement, as if they have forgotten that Jesus said, "For *I* am able to make you holy" (D&C 60:7; italics added), as if they have forgotten that perfection is a state reached in the eternities, not in mortality. Their efforts to force those around them into perfection often result in conflict, estrangement of family members, deep unhappiness, anger, and a sense of futility.

One facet of perfectionism is the need to control outcomes or results. It is the impulse behind repressive rules, which are designed to control outcomes or results in the lives of those around us, particularly children. It is, in human terms, an attempt at quality control.

The need to control springs from beliefs about the nature of man, beliefs that don't really reflect Gospel principles. For example, we may say we believe children to be pure in the sight of God, yet our parenting reflects a deep-rooted sense that it is up to us to *make* them do what is right. We may force them to go to church when they don't want to. We may manipulate them into taking part in an activity to which we are more committed than they are. We may monitor what they say, what friends they have, and what clothes they buy.

An example that is painful to me even now is what took place when I went shopping with my older daughter for her prom dress one year. We had looked in numerous shops with no luck. Finally, we drove to a mall we rarely patronized, and there she found the dress of her dreams. She looked like a young Grace Kelly in it, cool, elegant, beautiful. It was ice-blue with diagonal shirring on the bodice that came down to a flower of the same fabric at the waist. It was also sleeveless.

Relying on my interpretation of the teachings of the Church on modest dress, I refused to help her pay for it. It was the only dress she had seen in our long search that she liked, but I didn't budge. I forced her to try on others, including a pink dress with off-the-shoulder straps that could be pulled up across the shoulders for a more modest appearance. Since I wouldn't help her buy the blue dress, and since there was no time to look further, she capitulated.

She wore the pink dress to the prom, but it really wasn't very flattering. She knew it. I knew it. It has hung unused in the closet ever since. I still feel a bit sad about it. And I can still hear her argument: "Do you think I'm going to jump in bed just because I'm wearing a sleeveless dress? Can't you trust me to have better judgment than that?" My lack of trust in her judgment wasn't the issue: I was more concerned that her lack of adherence to a particular (but not a crucial) standard would make her a "bad" girl and me an unsuccessful Mormon mother.

Perfectionistic attitudes are fierce yardsticks for judgment. We say we should not judge, yet we often judge members of our church and the community by a pitiless standard of dress and behavior based on cultural opinions and monetary advantage. President Benson's classic address on pride left no doubt that we must cease judging others by externals and, if we must judge, strive to do so as Christ did, by what he saw in the heart.[2]

I sat in a Sunday School class one day listening to Church members discuss President Benson's talk. They were somewhat unsettled by it. In fact, they were trying to figure out how they could interpret it in such a way that they could feel justified continuing to live their lives in the spirit of competition and judgment. Why was it so hard for them (and for many others) to accept at face value what President Benson said?

It may be because we create a place for ourselves in the world through the process of judgment. We use culturally transmitted criteria to assign ourselves and others certain positions, roles, and importance. To let go of that would be to set ourselves adrift. We have not yet developed the intuition, the insight, or the depth of love required to live the sort of Zion life the prophet's talk exhorted us to live.

Perfectionism as a Stressor

As has already been mentioned, rigid, perfectionistic attitudes can cause dysfunction. Ann Wilson Schaef puts it this way in referring to organized religions in general:

> To be perfect, as defined by the institutional church, you not only have to have yourself under control, you also have everything and everyone else under control. Now this makes for an impossible dilemma. Since it is not possible for us to control absolutely our own lives — much less the lives of other people — striving to do so is a prescription for failure. Yet the church expects its members . . . to strive for perfection. If you should be able to and cannot, then you can only be a failure. Failure is depressing and perfectionists are depressed.[3]

Although most of us would say, "I know that nothing in life is perfect," many of us try very hard to make it so by living according to checklists of *shoulds* and *oughts*. Some of us carry the checklists in our heads, others in their daily planners. Whichever way we do it, our lists are extensive, and we typically compile them from several different sources. These sources include our family rules, principles of success as described in magazines and other popular literature, the prevailing culture, and our religion.

The shoulds and oughts we glean from religion include not only the commandments, but also "member teachings." John Turpin uses the term "member teachings" to designate standards of behavior that are *not* part of the gospel but are transmitted as part of American LDS culture. Some examples are, Good church members are conservative politically. Women are the homemakers (as if men have little part or voice in homemaking). Men should make enough to be the sole support of the household. Women should speak in sweet, soft voices. One Utah woman suggested a humorous example: Real Mormon women in Utah wear pink and blue.

The kinds of shoulds and oughts we have on our checklists differ according to the age and culture in which we live. Whether or not we are conscious of them, they profoundly affect not only our attitudes and behaviors, but also the way we feel about ourselves. In fact, the shoulds and oughts we are not conscious of have perhaps the stronger influence, precisely because we are not aware of them. For this reason, we will continue in the next chapter to look at the checklist.

CHAPTER 10

DOING THE CHECKLIST

Checklists are important. They are, in effect, the maps we use as we negotiate our way through life. They may be as simple as a few mental notes of things we need to do during the day, as practical as a written list of things to do that are checked off as each item is completed, as intangible as a set of internal, unspoken values by which we govern our actions, or as profound as journal entries describing one's goals and hopes for one's life. Not only do they contain information about cultural expectations and acceptable behavior, they also contain family rules and personal and business goals. We couldn't function without them.

However, checklists can also imprison. This is often the case when individuals never question the shoulds and oughts that have come from others, including God and the prophets. They therefore have no sense of having freely chosen them. They experience them as a burden that has been imposed from outside rather than a scheme of life-directing choices coming from inside. When that happens, individuals may either comply with the checklist resentfully or choose to rebel against it.

Of course, young children have no thoughts of questioning the checklists their parents and others give them—they don't even know they are internalizing one of their own. They tend to absorb what they see, hear, and feel — whether good or bad, true or untrue. Then they begin structuring their lives according to what they have absorbed. Only as they mature do they become aware that certain shoulds and oughts really may not be very positive or useful to them. At that point, they begin to question whether what they have learned is really true and right. As they continue to gain in experience, knowledge, and mental powers, they continue to question the checklist in light of the beliefs and values they are developing.

Some adults are disturbed over the idea that children may make up their own minds about important issues. A woman attending a seminar on how to establish Great Books study groups for grade-school children was surprised to learn the program philosophy, which is based on the belief that children can decide for themselves what a story means. In these groups, every opinion is valid, and the teacher does not draw a moral or lead the children to a foregone conclusion. This upset the woman greatly. She simply couldn't imagine letting children arrive at their own conclusions.

Parents who share this kind of thinking get understandably upset when their children — typically teenagers — begin to question what they have been taught. It can be a difficult time for both them and their children. However, in families where the adults do not feel threatened by a challenge to their values and the teenagers are secure in the knowledge that their feelings and thoughts will be validated, this can be a time of discovery and increased bonding for all concerned.

Unfortunately, this period of questioning is not encouraged or even allowed in some families. Teenagers in such a situation feel stifled. They may rebel in self-destructive ways, attempting to create a sense that they direct their own lives rather than that others direct them. Some teenagers may not rebel, taking instead a path of sullen compliance. Still others may cheerfully comply, convinced that their beliefs are exactly the same as their parents' beliefs. (In fact, they may very well be! It is interesting to note that when young people are allowed to question the internal checklist of shoulds and oughts based on parental values, they often discover that the values important to them are quite similar to those of their parents!)

Every individual must at some time or another begin to make his own value judgments and hold them up against the shoulds and oughts to see if that list is still valid for him personally. This process can and usually does last many years. In fact, the individual who examines his life regularly will always to some extent be reviewing his inner map in light of his beliefs and values. It is a positive and empowering activity. If we have (and are) engaged in this sort of internal audit, we have a sense that the checklist/map is one we have chosen. It comes from the inside, not the outside.

Going through this process is important, because there is a significant difference between directing one's life according to freely chosen values and principles and living by a checklist of others' expectations and values. The latter is what I refer to in the title of this chapter, "Doing the Checklist." When we "do the checklist," we use it to judge ourselves and others. We see our worth and our place in society as entirely dependent upon our accomplishing the things on the list.

The destructiveness of this stance is readily seen when the difference between self-worth and self-esteem is clearly drawn. Contrary to some popular usage, self-worth is not synonymous with self-esteem. Self-worth, which has to do with the intrinsic worth of the soul, is not hinged on accomplishment. Nothing we do or don't do can mar or destroy it. We are of value because we are eternal beings, intelligences who existed before the world was and who will have no end. Self-esteem, on the other hand,

71

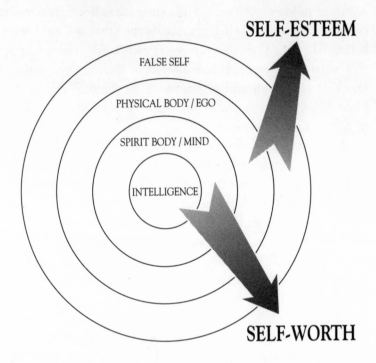

Self-esteem has its basis in image and accomplishment. It is therefore changeable. Self-worth has its basis in our eternal nature and is therefore not changeable.

is a feeling we get when we have accomplished something important to us or to others or when our actions are congruent with our beliefs.

Many of us who have grown up in dysfunctional families have little or no sense of self-worth. We thus depend on accomplishment to engender a feeling of self-esteem, hoping that it will fill the place made empty by feeling a lack of self-worth. When we are successful in checking off items on our list, we feel good about ourselves. When we fail, we are plunged into despair. Because we lack the stabilizing influence of a deep sense of self-worth, we spend our lives swinging back and forth between these two extremes.

The checklist thus encourages "black-and-white thinking." We can either check an item off, or we can't—it's an either/or situation (which is a logical fallacy called a false dilemma). We lose sight of the fact that for every situation there are more than two alternatives. We leave no room on the list for explanations of extenuating circumstances—we either succeed or we fail. Those caught up in this way of thinking have little sense of life as a process. They do not recognize the many points all along the continuum between success and failure.

Do the Checklist, *Or Else!*

When our sense of worth and esteem comes from the checklist, we end up putting more emphasis on the points on the list than on other values like trust and love. Not uncommonly, parents driven by perfectionism use force, manipulation, and even physical violence to assure the completion of the list.

Brother and Sister Sylvia decided together that they would accept the prophet's challenge to read the Book of Mormon daily. They decided to read immediately after the evening meal. But not all of their children agreed with this goal, in particular the oldest boy. He began disturbing the scripture-reading session. Brother Sylvia tried to maintain order, but he could see that if things continued the way they were going, the family could not meet their goal.

One particular evening, the son was so disruptive that Brother Sylvia picked him up and bodily threw him into his room. He slammed the door shut, stomped back into the kitchen, and asked another child to continue reading. That child, disturbed by the violence she had just witnessed, refused. The scripture-reading program ended in chaos.

"Doing the checklist" can set up a destructive cycle, as is

obvious from the story of the Sylvia family. Father Leo Booth describes this vicious cycle: "In many homes . . . we see a hypocritical lifestyle. The yearning for physical, mental and spiritual perfection is often followed by bouts of anger, violence, and sexual abuse, followed by guilt, remorse and self-pity. Again nothing is said."[1]

Individuals caught up in this kind of cycle set goals for themselves and their families. They work hard at trying to accomplish them, but they feel as if they are not achieving the success they should. They respond by venting their frustration in abusive behavior, then feeling guilty because they have "lost it."

I believe this cycle is familiar to most if not all of us, for the severity of the mood swings and the way in which the frustration is acted out can range from mild to severe. The true failure has not so much to do with missing our stated goal as with the fact that we have lost sight of the principles that govern relationships: individual worth, freedom to choose, and the power of love to influence for good.

Perfectionism Is Hostile to the Gospel

A perfectionistic system creates dysfunction because it denies individuals the five freedoms Virginia Satir speaks of: the freedom to freely think what one thinks, to feel what one feels, to choose what one wants, to respond to the present as one perceives it, and to decide what one wants to be. It demands a false, people-, and God-pleasing self and thus creates a deep sense of shame. This is another aspect of the unhealthy, or toxic, shame described in chapter seven.

Toxic shame makes a mockery of the Atonement. It makes us feel as if *we* are what's wrong, as if, deep down inside, we are irrevocably faulty, with no redeeming or redeemable qualities whatever. It makes us feel as if the self that we really are is not and can never be acceptable and would certainly be rejected by both man and God if it were ever revealed. Toxic shame makes us feel unworthy of what we most need: love and acceptance. Most importantly, it cuts us off from feeling the loving, supportive presence of our Heavenly Father.

Perfectionistic systems, whether personal, as in families, or impersonal, as in organizations, often seek to motivate by criticizing, guilting, and shaming, exactly the kind of behaviors that cause toxic shame. Individuals belonging to these systems typically create false selves to protect themselves from the pain of feeling ashamed and unworthy. The false self can be very acceptable to organizations and society in general, for its main function is to please. But because it is a lie by its very nature, it can never be acceptable to our Father in Heaven. For this reason, nothing could be more antagonistic to the gospel of Jesus Christ than perfectionism.

In contrast to this, the gospel teaches that we are children of God, eternal beings of infinite worth. It acknowledges the fact that we will make mistakes, that we sometimes will have negative thoughts and feelings, that we will have desires contrary to the laws and will of God. Nowhere in the scriptures are we told that the solution is to pretend that we don't experience any of the above. In fact, they tell us the exact opposite, that it is important to know ourselves. (See, for example, Ps. 77:6; Prov. 14:8; 20:27; Lam. 3:40.) When we acknowledge what we really think and what we really feel, we are able to base our subsequent actions and decisions on truth. If we do not, we end up basing our actions and decisions on the false self, and spiritual progress and assistance from the Spirit is blocked.

True change in a gospel context is possible because individuals feel accepted and loved by their Father in Heaven. They learn that if they make mistakes, they can repent, and God will forgive and forget those mistakes. Supported by these positive feelings, they are open to new information, which presents them with a wide range of alternatives to their behavior, some of which they might not have been aware of previously. Not only that, because they feel secure in their worth, they feel more capable of making new choices and carrying them through.

It is not unusual, however, for people to prefer to busily polish aspects of their false, people-, and God-pleasing selves, rather than do the work necessary to prepare themselves for deep transforming spiritual change. The crux of that preparation is self-realization — knowing who they really are — and self-realization involves sometimes painful emotional work. However, that task is required of all of us, and the sooner we begin, the sooner we will reap the rewards of increased joy, love, and spirituality.

CHAPTER 11

CODEPENDENCE IN LATTER-DAY SAINT SOCIETY

The hidden rules of codependence can manifest themselves in any system, whether a family, an institution, or society itself. LDS society is no exception. John C. Turpin gives an example in his tape *Codependency: What It Is and How to Reduce It within a Gospel Context.* He quotes an LDS woman who says, "I believe the LDS woman must not be selfish, she must do what's asked, keep smiling (after all, the woman sets the tone in the family), love unconditionally, sacrifice, protect, and at all costs hide the hurt."[1] Her words paint a perfect picture of codependent attitudes. Another LDS woman was asked by an aunt at a family gathering, "How are you?" But the aunt didn't wait for her response. She said, "Of course you're all right. You have to be."

Naturally, not all LDS women perceive their role in the same way as the women in those examples. For instance, several women I spoke to had never heard the phrase, "The woman sets the tone in the home." Others, including men, had been taught it over and over again not only by teachers in church organizations, but also by articles in national magazines and the family section of newspapers.

Although the attitudes revealed in the woman's words may not seem unusual, you may be surprised at how similar they are to attitudes common among women with alcoholic husbands. Marie Schutt enumerates them in her book *Wives of Alcoholics:*

1. Peace at any price
2. Maintain the conspiracy of silence
3. Never quit
4. Never discuss feelings
5. Try to seem normal[2]

When I read this list to a woman in our stake, her eyes filled with tears. She said, "That sounds just like my mother." More than one woman had the same response, for these attitudes are prevalent among us. They are particularly common among women, but many men also hold to them. For that reason, considering the effect they have on our relationships is important.

Peace at Any Price

The woman who believes that she must keep peace in her family pays a heavy price in terms of her own integrity. She always defers to the one holding the power (most often but not always her husband). She doesn't express her true feelings about issues, because to do so might cause trouble. She denies her wants and needs in order to fill others' expectations, regardless of how out-of-line they are. She often allows herself to be emotionally and verbally, if not physically, abused.

The consequences of this attitude are serious. For one thing, the children do not see their parents in helpful parenting models and may learn codependent behavior themselves. For instance, children who do not see their parents resolve differences of opinion or conflict through communication and compromise may not learn how to handle disagreement except by denying it.

For another, adults who force themselves to acquiesce often

turn to deadening activities so that they will not feel the pain of denying their own interests or values. A woman might read hundreds of romance novels or eat huge amounts of food. Conversely, she may starve herself as a means of asserting some control over her life. A man might spend all his free time watching sports or detective programs. He might immerse himself in church work, in business, or in a hobby. At the worst, both children and adults in such a family may be victims of escalating emotional and physical abuse.

Maintain the Conspiracy of Silence

The conspiracy of silence refers to keeping a family secret like the loss of employment, an institutionalized family member, mental illness, or an unwanted pregnancy. This rule is most destructive when the secret is abuse, particularly physical or sexual abuse. The conspiracy of silence often creates deep feelings of worthlessness, shame, and helplessness in the victim. It is potentially dangerous and, in the case of abuse, may even be life-threatening. In addition, it creates destructive patterns in other family members who feel compelled to maintain silence.

The conspiracy of silence is both a family rule and a cultural rule. In terms of abuse, the conspiracy of silence primarily affects women and children. These victims of emotional, physical, or sexual abuse often do not feel that they can ask for and receive appropriate help. Although general awareness of abuse issues has increased markedly, most people are highly uncomfortable around victims. They do not want to hear what has happened.

Unfortunately, this feeling also exists among some Church members, even among those holding leadership positions. Because they do not want to know about or are unprepared to deal with such situations, they ignore the signs and/or they discount the stories.

This is illustrated by the experience of "Jane," an LDS woman whose husband was physically abusive. "Jane" told her story in the *Exponent II* issue on abuse, relating that many of her ward members didn't believe what she told them about her situation. Distressed by their lack of understanding, she searched for possible explanations of their attitudes. She wrote:

> I was so confused by this behavior myself that I have read a great deal about what teachers and psychologists call the "search for cognitive consistency." . . .
>
> We all need order in our worlds. We structure that order by setting up categories and putting things in them so that they make sense. . . . Basically what happens is that once we set up our categories and establish an orderly way to organize reality, we have some peace. . . . We are disturbed, however, when information comes along that doesn't fit our sense of peace and order. . . .
>
> If we have a category in our minds for what we see as the behavior of a good LDS person/priesthood-holder and that category doesn't include a place for the possibility of abusive behavior, we take the easiest road and throw out the report of such behavior.[3]

Another way some people skirt the issue of abuse is to blame the victim. While General Authorities have come out strongly against any kind of abuse in the home, the dynamics of abusive relationships are still not understood very well. And even some educated, enlightened leaders can hold assumptions that prompt them to put the responsibility of the abuse on the victim and to go easy on the abuser.

In one case, a woman was beaten by her husband. She told her bishop, who said, "Stop making him so mad." In another case, a woman had told those in authority over a period of years that she was being abused. They did nothing for her. After one attack, she asked the police to put out a restraining order, barring her husband from the house. They tried to reach him throughout the day but were unable to until evening—they served him with the order in the middle of a church meeting. It was no doubt an excruciating moment for all concerned, but the comment of a church leader revealed that he was more concerned for the public image of both the man himself and the Church in general than for the safety of the woman. He said, "How could you embarrass him so?" (I have included this disturbing story to show how an uninformed response can add a second level of abuse to someone who is already victimized. It is a single example and is not meant to be taken as a reflection of the attitude of stake presidents and bishops in general.)

Not only do others often blame the victim, the victims also very often blame themselves. They feel responsible for their husbands' rages or attacks. They assume, for example, that if they weren't so slow (or clumsy, ineffective, uneducated, disorganized), their husbands would stop hitting them. Such beliefs keep many women in destructive marriages.

To be perfectly clear, the conspiracy of silence is not the same as being careful about when and how you confide personal problems to others, which is an issue of appropriateness. The conspiracy of silence is a collusion between members of a group to ignore something that should be dealt with.

In a story reminiscent of "The Emperor's New Clothes," a group of people sit around the dining-room table, eating a meal. In the middle of the table lies a dead horse. These people eat, drink, and converse as if nothing is wrong, for they have tacitly agreed to ignore the presence of the horse. Someone from outside the group joins them and cries out, "What's going on here! How can you pretend to enjoy your meal when there's a dead horse on the dining-room table?" The others, having agreed to ignore the horse, accuse him of being crazy and go on eating.

81

Although steps are currently being taken to raise awareness of abuse issues in the Church, it is for some members still very much the dead horse on the dining-room table.

The "Never" Fallacies

Never quit. While the concept of eternal marriage is of paramount importance to us as Church members, we ought to also acknowledge that there is no virtue in staying in a destructive relationship of emotional or verbal abuse. Women and children are not required to put themselves at risk.

The never-quit cultural and codependent rule causes many women and men to feel as if they have no choice but to suffer in a loveless or abusive marriage. This was the situation of Charlotte, as reported by Ellen Goodman. An LDS woman living in Salt Lake City, Charlotte was enduring a marriage in which both her husband and her children continuously devalued her. She wanted things to be different, but she felt helpless to make changes. Goodman wrote:

> Charlotte . . . looks at past choices as obligations to endure. She doesn't really believe that she can make a change in the rules or the regulations of her life. In fact, as we talked, she told me I was the first person to ask her whether she was happy since her father had died. . . . Charlotte, when asked by her neighbors if she didn't think she deserved better, replied, "Personally, I don't. I can't think of anything I deserve."[4]

In many such marriages, improving relationships is not even an option since the other spouse either denies that problems exist or refuses to enter into therapy of any kind. Or, in an example of "black-and-white thinking," the spouse cannot see any choices other than continuing on in the abusive situation or getting a divorce. Whenever one woman tried to bring up issues important

82

to her, her husband's response was "Do you want a divorce?" Of course, she didn't—what she wanted was a better relationship. Her husband's attitude left her with empty hands.

Never discuss feelings. This rule is detrimental to everyone in the family. Children learn to invalidate their emotions, to live the lie that "I'm all right. Everything's cool. We don't have any problems." No one feels free to express themselves honestly. True communication is impossible in such a situation.

Feelings are not right or wrong in and of themselves. They are, rather, indicators of something we need to explore and take care of. They can be a response to some current event or to unresolved issues from the past. When we acknowledge them and express them appropriately, we respond to events in our lives honestly. When we suppress them, we set ourselves up for outbursts of rage or other inappropriate behavior or for depression. We perpetuate the false self. Men often respond to this dictum by working harder, staying busy, or getting depressed. Women often respond to it by getting sick or depressed.

In some families, this rule is expanded to read, *Never discuss anything that doesn't fit the family's accepted image.* Anything that is out of step with the way the parents want their family to be is simply ignored. The parents do not speak to their children about their problems, even when they are aware of them. Rather, they withdraw their love and support, which makes life even more difficult for the children. They intend for it to be more difficult, hoping by that means to bring their children back into line.

One son was working through a relatively minor issue involving personal worthiness. He had taken the steps necessary to do so but felt that it was appropriate to forego taking the sacrament for a time. His parents noticed this. Instead of asking him in an atmosphere of support and love if they could do anything to help him out, they withdrew into silence.

83

As a result, they suffered unnecessarily, imagining all sorts of reasons for his failure to partake. They could easily have made a "reality check" by simply asking their son if they could help him with anything. Of course, the young man may not have chosen to go into detail about his situation, but he could have reassured them concerning his efforts to put things right.

He also suffered unnecessarily. Instead of experiencing the outpouring of love and support that might have resulted from such a conversation with his parents, he experienced a withdrawal of love and support. His parents rule of silence prevented him from even bringing up the subject.

Never allow problems to show outside the family. In a healthy family suffering a transient difficulty, keeping up appearances may be a way of moving on. In an unhealthy family, trying to seem normal goes hand in hand with the conspiracy of silence. It keeps the secret. It perpetuates the lie. It freezes the family in pain. The try-to-seem-normal rule says that appearances are reality: If you keep up appearances, everything is okay. Family members often hold to this rule with such vehemence that they become convinced that indeed everything is okay. If one brave individual decides to tell it like it is, the others will probably tell him that he's imagining things. "What do you mean? Everything's going fine. You must be nuts." Such a situation breaks down integrity and breeds hypocrisy.

No wonder therapists and people in recovery programs often call such situations "crazy-making." If you see that the emperor is naked or that there is a dead horse on the dining-room table but everyone tells you that you're mistaken, you might begin to have doubts yourself.

CHAPTER 12

EFFECTS OF DYSFUNCTION

The effects of growing up in dysfunctional families are far-reaching. As has been mentioned, family members typically take on rigid roles to meet the demands of the system. In doing so, they abdicate their right to make choices about who and what they want to be. They have difficulty expressing or acknowledging their feelings, thoughts, and needs. Congruence — the state in which one's actions are an expression of one's values — is frequently foreign to them because they may not have any idea what their own values are. They depend on others to tell them what is important and what they should do.

Such individuals usually do not know what normal behavior is like. Because they have never seen models of healthy interaction, they don't know the ways in which husbands and wives can work together, deal with conflict, and be emotionally intimate. They may not know how to make choices between alternatives because they have never believed that they have options to choose from. They do not know how to state what they want because they have invalidated their own wants for so long that they don't even know what they are.

Every Christmas season in hundreds of thousands of houses

all across the U.S.A., a codependency drama unfolds. Wives and husbands ask each other what they want for Christmas. The answer is "I don't want anything." Despite cajoling and repeated questioning, the spouses stoutly maintain that there is nothing they desire. They may feel noble and altruistic, thinking that they're not materially minded, but the truth more often is that they have disregarded their wants and needs for so long, they couldn't say what they wanted if they had to!

The flip side can also be true. Adult children may also have excessive demands. Such people have no trouble writing out long lists of what they need and want to "be happy" and "feel loved." The sad truth is that all their efforts are misdirected into making and fulfilling checklists, and they are left still feeling empty. As Dennis Wholey explained, "Adult children never learn to love themselves, and as grown-ups, they are confused, hopeless, and despairing. Adult children do not get positive messages in childhood and often spend a life-time searching for affirmation and validation as adults."[1]

Not only are the children of an unhealthy family affected, the next generation is affected as well. A person who was reared in such a family may often be drawn to another with whom they can replay or recreate the conditions they grew up in. Why? Because they know what the rules are in those conditions, and they know what is required of them. And they may not know any other way of relating. Oddly, they feel comfortable in dysfunctional relationships.

The scriptures that speak of the sins of the parents being visited upon the children (see Ex. 20:5; 34:7) is clearly applicable to the way dysfunction is passed down through the generations. I have devised the following schematic that illustrates the common sequence of events:

1. Children of dysfunctional families are not allowed to feel their own emotions or make their own

86

choices. Their parents can't meet their needs. They are emotionally abandoned.

❖

2. They develop what John Bradshaw calls a "hole in the soul."[2] They become dependent on some person, some substance, some activity, or some system to give them a sense of connectedness and occasional relief from pain.

❖

3. They thus develop addictive or compulsive behaviors to plug the "hole in the soul."

❖

4. They enter into new codependent or dysfunctional relationships in which they recycle the things they learned in their own families about interrelating and dealing with stress.

❖

5. When they marry and have children, they create another dysfunctional family. Never having had their own needs met, they do not know how to meet the needs of their children. If they were victims of some level of abuse as children, they often become perpetrators.

❖

6. A new generation of abused, abandoned children go through life with a "hole in the soul."

This cycle typically goes on from generation to generation until someone decides, "Enough! The cycle must be broken." The dysfunction continues until someone decides to do the necessary work of healing oneself and encourage his or her children and loved ones to also do so.

Common Adult Children Characteristics

Children of dysfunctional families grow up to be "adult children," a designation that may at first seem to be a contradiction in terms. Such individuals are adult in stature and have adult responsibilities, but their emotional development has been blocked in significant ways. The phrase currently refers to persons who have experienced some sort of dysfunctional family relationships in their childhood.

Janet Woititz lists some of the characteristics of adult children in general. While individuals from healthy homes may see themselves in one or more statements, those from dysfunctional homes will be able to identify with many, if not all, of them.

1. Adult children guess at what normal is.
2. Adult children have trouble following a project through to the end.
3. Adult children lie when it would be just as easy to tell the truth.
4. Adult children judge themselves without mercy.
5. Adult children have difficulty having fun.
6. Adult children take themselves very seriously.
7. Adult children have difficulty with intimate relationships.
8. Adult children overreact to changes over which they have no control.
9. Adult children constantly seek approval and affirmation.
10. Adult children usually feel different from other people.
11. Adult children are super responsible or super irresponsible.
12. Adult children are extremely loyal, even in the face of evidence that the loyalty is undeserved.
13. Adult children tend to lock themselves into a course of action without giving serious consideration to alternative behavior or possible consequences. This impulsiveness leads to confusion, self-loathing, and loss of control over their environment. As a result, they spend tremendous amounts of time cleaning up the mess.

As you were reading these characteristics, how many caused a recognition response, an "Aha!" or an "Oh, no!"? Sometimes people who grew up in dysfunctional families first recognize the fact when they realize that such lists accurately describe many of their own feelings, attitudes, and behaviors. Something like this is sometimes needed to help those recognize the truth who have minimized or denied the circumstances of their youth, especially if physical or sexual abuse was involved.

In such cases, even when the individuals do finally recognize that they were abused, they may not be able to face the truth or talk about particular incidents. Getting to that point is often a lengthy process that can only be worked through with appropriate support.

The fact that healing can't be accomplished in isolation is reflected in the words of Grete Peterson: "The Savior is the ultimate healer, but that does not mean that there is no pain or that solutions come easily. We need each other to move the healing process along, acknowledging the reality of abuse, and our communal vulnerability begins to move us toward wholeness."[3] The way we begin the journey "toward wholeness" is the subject of the second part of this book.

PART 2

THE HEALING PROCESS

CHAPTER 13

THREE BASIC GUIDELINES

If you have seen yourself in some of the previous pages, you may have been impatient to get to this part of the book, the "How to" or "Fix it" section. Before you read further, knowing certain things about what you will be encountering next is important.

1. There is no quick fix.

For those of us in dysfunctional families, the way we react to dysfunction (and attendant abuse) has influenced how we look at every aspect of the world. It has defined every issue we have, whether in relationships, self-esteem, employment, or any other part of our lives.

Working through these issues is not a one-time thing. It is a lifetime proposition, part of working out our salvation. This may sound discouraging, but giving in to despair only puts us back at the beginning, and starting over and over again is a painful waste of time. A more helpful attitude is to remember that every time we deal with a reoccurrence of a destructive family pattern, our abilities increase, and we come that much closer to establishing a healthier, happier family. Then, as the peaks and valleys of our lives become less severe, life in general will become more pleasant and productive.

2. Outside help is necessary.

Dealing with the issues relating to dysfunction is difficult and emotionally draining. Rarely can an individual undertake the healing process alone. There are several reasons for this:

A. We typically have a great many unacknowledged emotions about our childhood. Acknowledging and releasing them is not likely unless we are working with a therapist or in a group that provides a safe place for us to do so.

B. We have not experienced what healthy relationships can be like, so we need someone to model them and point out what aspects of our family patterns were or are destructive.

C. We need an outside perspective to help us discover what aspects of our thinking patterns keep us stuck in destructive behaviors. We also need help to learn how to restructure family patterns. In addition to therapists, books and classes—those offered through community education or HMOs, for example—can help.

D. If our situations are such that we are in danger, we need help to change it. That may mean seeking shelter, and it may mean taking legal action. We need the support, encouragement, and advice from those who work with abuse issues in order to make the appropriate response.

3. There is no set formula.

Since each person's experience is different, the way he or she approaches the healing process will also be different. However, there are some general steps that apply to all. I have outlined them here and presented some activities that support each step. These activities are designed to give you some idea of the process as a whole and to get you started. Many of them can be done on an individual basis, but some sort of support is recommended.

A. *Facing the facts* — acknowledging the unpleasant events of childhood and their effects.

B. *Feeling the feelings* — responding to the repressed emotions surrounding childhood abuse.

C. *Forgiving* — forgiving the child we were for being too to small to protect us, and perhaps forgiving our abuser.

D. *Getting help/helping others* — learning how to ask for appropriate help, taking action to prevent abuse, and learning how to find strength in helping others.

E. *Reconnecting* — doing activities that reacquaint us with all aspects of our selves.

F. *Reparenting* — giving ourselves the things we needed from our parents, but did not receive.

G. *Releasing* — letting go of negative thought patterns, destructive ways of relating, and unrealistic expectations.

H. *Restructuring* — learning (perhaps for the first time) the correct principles of interrelating.

J. *Creating a daily program* — establishing a program that supports these healing activities and attitudes.

The above steps are presented as an effective healing process for those in pain. It is also an effective personal growth process of those who feel generally comfortable with their lives but who wish to make changes in a given area.

CHAPTER 14

FACING THE FACTS

Typically, members of dysfunctional families seek to solve their problems, to get out of the pain, by doing the checklist more determinedly. They hope that getting complete control of their lives will bring them happiness at last, or at least alleviate the hurt.

They may think, for example, that by upping their average morning family scripture reading from four to six days a week, things will be better. They may take on more callings. They may become stricter in what they will allow their children to do on Sunday. They may fast for inordinate periods of time. They may strive for more business success. They may work harder at polishing the family image they present to the public. Caught in the codependent trap, members of dysfunctional families embark on fruitless efforts to do it right.

The lucky ones learn finally that doing more and doing it faster and doing it better will not solve their problems or bring the changes they long for. (Even members of healthy families face certain problems that can't be solved simply by trying harder.) They learn that the checklist, in and of itself, has no power to save. They learn that scripture reading and prayer alone won't make their family strong if dysfunctional behavior—including abuse—is the norm in their household. Paradoxically, relief comes from doing *less* and doing it *differently,* not by doing more.

What steps can we take to achieve our goal of family happiness, then?

First, we stop identifying ourselves primarily by what we are *doing* and begin the difficult, sometimes frightening, but ultimately exciting and fulfilling work of identifying ourselves by what we are *being.* We begin the process of knowing ourselves, both the self that lives and moves on this earth and the self that lived and moved with God in the premortal existence.

For adult children, this can be the hardest step. They may be incapable of truly knowing either aspect of self until they stop ignoring the pain of the past and avoiding the truth about their childhood. Joan Phene writes:

> It's important for people to know the truth about their families. Therapy is not about "Oh, weren't Mom and Dad horrible." There can be some of that for a limited amount of time . . . but [what] most adult children need [is] to identify what happened to them and understand how that affects their thinking, their relationships, their work and their view of the world. People make progress as they understand the consequences of their past and begin to have some empathy for that child who grew up in that situation.[1]

Therefore, facing the truth about what growing up or being in a dysfunctional home means is the first step. In many ways it is like dealing with the grief of a terminal illness. The emotional stages one goes through are similar to the steps of grief Elizabeth Kübler-Ross describes in her book *On Death and Dying,*[2] some of which are discussed in this and following chapters. Note, however, that the sequence one experiences is not fixed, nor is there any usual time frame.

Denial

At first, most children from dysfunctional families want to deny or discount what their lives were like for them as children. Denial is the means they use to protect both their parents and themselves. They protect their parents by continuing to live the lie, "Our family was all right." They don't want to have to confront parents with the truth of how negatively their past has affected them.

Many victims of abuse are told, "You can't say anything about this—it would kill your mother!" Others may never hear those words, yet they have the feeling that telling the truth would destroy everyone and everything around them. Some victims do tell, only to find that the whole family rejects their story. The family members' need to retain the belief in the "happy family" is so great that accusing the victim of being mistaken is easier than facing the truth.

Adult children may also deny the truth because they fear abandonment, feeling that if they tell the truth, their parents will reject them. They do not recognize that this is paradoxical, since part of their pain comes from the fact that adult children have already been emotionally abandoned by their parents. The children were not nourished, affirmed, or encouraged to be themselves.

Coming to the conclusion "My parents didn't love me," or "They didn't love me enough," or "They weren't able to love me" is horribly painful. This is one of the reasons that victims so often feel responsible for the violence done to them. As small children, they feel that they must believe in the love of their parents, so the explanation they typically devise for the abuse is that they were bad, that they did something to deserve it. Women who are victims of violence often hold to their belief in their husbands' love by using the same logic, "I must have done something to make him mad."

A college-age student was told by his therapist that he was the victim of physical abuse. Their one-sided conversation went like this:

> "Well, part of it was my fault. I shouldn't have been so stubborn."
> "No. It wasn't your fault."
> "I should have done what they told me."
> "Maybe. But it wasn't your fault."
> "I really was a pain in the butt. I knew how to get at my old man."
> "You don't get it, do you? It *wasn't your fault*."

The lesson is an important one. As a whole, society has yet to make some changes in its assumptions about abuse and violence, because it still places blame, even in part, on the victim.

Breaking out of denial is especially difficult for adult children who have good childhood memories along with the bad. Only after honest evaluation of the way their past affects their present can they finally say, "Yes, I was a victim of abuse. My family was dysfunctional." Then they must be careful not to discount that admission with a phrase like "But it wasn't that bad." If the abuse of childhood has affected the course of their lives and all of their relationships, it *was* that bad. They must realize that they need not reject the good memories to be able to face the truth.

For Latter-day Saints especially, shame over admitting to a much-less-than-perfect family or marriage can make denial a particularly difficult stage to get out of. One of the purposes I had for writing this book was to give those in pain permission or a way to be open about their suffering. We who come from dysfunctional families are not intrinsically defective. Neither are we unworthy. But we are wounded and in pain, and we need to be healed.

Acknowledging What Happened and How We Feel about It

The change from denial to acknowledgment of the truth about childhood is not an academic exercise — although it may start out that way. The first step that adult children may have to take is just saying the words, "I was abused as a child. I grew up in a dysfunctional home." Realizing the feelings they have suppressed as a result of their childhood will probably take longer. And when they come, these feelings can be profoundly disturbing: rage, fear, the feeling of being annihilated. They are not everyday, routine feelings. They well up like a howl from a black hole somewhere inside.

Acknowledging what happened in the past can be particularly difficult for victims of sexual abuse if their way of surviving was to repress all memory of it. In such cases, their body remembers, even if their mind doesn't. Without knowing why, they may be suffering from depression, from misdirected rage, from panic attacks. Some victims know only indirectly that they were abused, because in the course of seeking help for the problems described above, they recognized themselves in lists of behaviors characteristic of victims of child sexual abuse.

An interesting example is that of a woman who was hospitalized for tests because of physical problems. Her doctor asked her how she was feeling. She replied, "I'm *angry,* and I don't know why or what to do about it."

The doctor's next question was "Were you sexually abused as a child?"

Astonished, she replied, "Yes! But how did you know?"

"I didn't know, but whenever I have women patients in their

thirties experiencing a lot of anger, it usually has to do with an incident of abuse they have not resolved."

As I write this, I am aware that these stories are all of women victims. Not all victims are women, but male victims typically do not reveal what happened to them or seek help in dealing with it. Thus, most literature on child sexual abuse is written for women, and most groups for survivors of sexual abuse are for women. This is unfortunate, for it is quite difficult for male victims to find a support system for working through sexual abuse issues.

CHAPTER 15

FEELING THE FEELINGS

Adult children of dysfunctional families experience a range of strong, oftentimes profoundly disturbing emotions when they begin to confront their past. However, acknowledging and facing those emotions are necessary parts of the healing process. This is not as easy as one might think. Our understanding of emotions and the role they play in our lives is limited. To many people, in fact, they remain a great mystery.

In general, we do not quite know what to do with our emotions. Some feel them but dismiss their importance. Some feel them with the romanticist's excess and assign them too much importance. Some fear feeling them so much that they ignore or discount them. Still others have put so much energy into controlling and repressing their feelings that they no longer are aware of having particular feelings about anything.

These responses show a lack of understanding of the true role emotions play in our lives. They are extremely important, for they teach us much about ourselves, the world around us, and our relationship to other human beings. For instance, positive emotions tell us something is right — we feel joyful, peaceful, content, expansive, loving. Negative emotions tell us something is wrong—we feel fearful, angry, sad, hopeless. They tell us when something needs to be changed, and not necessarily something outside of ourselves, such as another person's behavior. Even our spirituality is based to a degree on emotion: a burning in the bosom, a feeling of peace or love, the sense that something is right for reasons that have nothing to do with logic.

Once we are aware of a negative feeling in regard to a particular circumstance, it is up to us to appropriately express what we feel to the individual(s) concerned. This is a skill that takes some study and practice. We generally do not talk directly to the person we are angry at, for example. We act as if nothing is wrong, then burst into anger at a spouse or child.

A more appropriate response is to address the issue using what psychologists call "I messages." We state what has upset us, how it makes us feel, and what we would like to see changed. When we do so, we acknowledge our feelings and needs positively. Even if the result is not all we want, we gain considerable relief from having expressed ourselves. Often, our greatest need is simply to have our viewpoint acknowledged. When that happens, the power behind the negative emotion dissipates to a great extent.

This process of dealing with emotion can be called "keeping current." We acknowledge emotions as they arise and take appropriate action, whether it is addressing the issue with others or making a change in ourselves. We might think of current emotions—emotions unattached to past pain—as "fresh" or "healthy." The kinds of emotions, however, that we as adult children are dealing with are not fresh or healthy. They are old emotions, long held. They are toxic emotions.

Such destructive emotions got that way through a long process, beginning in our childhood. How many children feel they can tell a parent that they are angry for being emotionally or physically abused? How many can say, "I'm hurt! I don't feel

103

loved?" A junior-high girl ran away from home for just those reasons. When she was discovered and brought back, her parents had a long session with her in the bedroom. They wanted to know why she had run away from home, but she never told them because honest communication had never been encouraged in her home. She feared her parents' reaction if she told the truth.

So as children, we began "stuffing" our feelings, pushing them down inside us, disregarding them, or masking them. But they didn't disappear. Every time a situation similar to the one that caused the original pain occurs, that old pain surfaces, combining with the new. It prompts us to react defensively, usually in a way that hurts either ourselves or others. Typically, no resolution is reached in such situations, for instead of dealing with the issues at hand, we recite our litany of grievances, sometimes going back years! Because nothing is resolved, we are still vulnerable. The only thing that has happened is that our negative emotions have been once more reinforced.

When we keep recycling rather than releasing our negative emotions, we suffer. Some of us turn ourselves into human pressure cookers. As the pressure of our negative emotions rises, we let off steam by lashing out, often toward people and situations unrelated to what is really bothering us. (We may not even know what is really bothering us if we have repressed our feelings and/or blotted out certain memories.) Others of us get sick. We may suffer painful headaches, colitis, or even autoimmune illnesses such as asthma, allergies, and arthritis. We may become chronically depressed. Whatever the outward manifestation, the inward state is the same: we are clogged with emotions that have not been resolved. Emotionally, we have not moved past the events of our childhood.

As we can see, learning how to deal with emotions associated with past events is important. We need to learn how to express them in a manner and in a situation that will ultimately be helpful, not harmful. Unfortunately, people sometimes misunderstand what is meant by feeling and releasing emotions. They take such words as permission to indulge in uncontrolled rage leading to emotionally or physically abusive behavior. This is not what "Feeling the Feelings" is about. Nor is it an invitation to get stuck in emotional excess, which sometimes happens when people become addicted either to the emotions themselves or to the attention they receive when they tell their story.

Feeling the feelings is a freeing stage of the process. Adult children who have worked through it to a certain extent often feel suddenly more open, expansive, even physically lighter. They may also feel a surge of energy. This happens because they are no longer carrying the heavy burden of repressed emotions or using so much of their energy to control their feelings. They are free to direct this newly available energy into other, more satisfying endeavours.

Having set this groundwork, we will now focus on two of the emotions adult children need to work through and work out, anger and grief. Then we will discuss moving toward forgiveness.

Anger

Anger is not a socially acceptable emotion. We are taught to bridle our anger. Men often channel it into aggressive behavior. Women often channel it into more acceptable emotions. For instance, women who were taught not to express anger often cry instead. Given the general lack of experience in handling anger appropriately, it is not surprising that adult children feel threatened when they begin to experience this feeling.

Typically, when they allow themselves to acknowledge their anger, a huge amount of it is unleashed. This is typically true of victims of sexual or physical abuse. "How could you do this to me!" they rage. They frequently feel extremely bitter toward those in authority, for such people represent the adult authority figures

105

who should have protected and nurtured them when they were small.

Victims are often terrified when these powerful emotions begin to surface. They attempt to push them back down, fearful that they and others around them will be destroyed. They describe what they are experiencing with words like "volcano" or "whirlwind." Only in settings and with people they completely trust do they feel safe enough to begin dealing with such strong feelings. Most turn to therapists and groups working with similar issues.

Sometimes acting anger out in nondestructive ways helps — beating a bed with a tennis racquet or smashing empty cans with a baseball bat, for instance. In her seminar "Becoming a Survivor," Lynda N. Driscoll says of her experience dealing with sexual abuse, "You have to be at last angry, enraged at the wrong done to you. We are told often that we shouldn't be angry . . . but I had to get the anger out so I could let love in. Among other things, I spent a lot of time with hot angry tears, yelling and even swearing at my dead father. I even found it helpful, if somewhat hazardous to my reputation, to go into the forest and beat the heck out of dead trees."[1]

Sometimes writing in a journal or writing letters helps. One pours out all the vitriol in journal passages that may never be read by others or letters that may never be sent. Certainly, victims of any kind of abuse will need to consider carefully whether or not to share such passages or send such letters to their abuser. While confronting abusers can be a helpful and healthy thing to do, such a confrontation — even by means of the written word — must be thought out carefully. In personal confrontations, much consideration must be given as to the setting, the parameters of what will be allowed, and the results desired.

The necessity of feeling emotions puts some adult children in a Catch-22 situation. They have stuggled for years to control negative feelings by refusing to acknowledge them. Now they

106

must allow them in all their messiness, ugliness, and heat. The problem seems on the surface to be different for adult children whose own uncontrolled anger and rage have resulted in abusive behavior toward others. But for both groups the task is similar: to identify the issues and the deeper emotions underlying their reactions to certain situations and to learn new, more appropriate forms of behavior.

For those who have repressed their emotions over a long period of time, learning to acknowledge them is not easy. Some may try to avoid doing so by intellectualizing. They say, "Yes, yes, I know what happened. Now let's get on with learning how to deal with it." By which they mean: Tell me what to read, what to say, and how to act. Give me a plan to follow so I won't have to feel. As one adult child put it, "What we want is drive-through therapy."

It won't work. Healing is promoted by finally allowing the full expressions of feelings. Emotional feelings, according to one author, have a pathway much like the neurological pathway that physical feelings have.[2] When some event initiates them, they begin to flow down the pathway. If allowed to complete their flow, they dissipate to some extent. If they are blocked, they increase in power and have an effect on the physical body as well as the mind. That is why it is important to learn to recognize what emotion we are feeling and stay with it as long as possible. The longer a person can stay with it, allow it, and experience it, the less power it will have when it demands attention later on.

Finally, anger can be used as a source of energy to fuel positive action. At some point in the healing process, victims may direct this energy into an advocacy program, for example. Doing so gives them a sense of power because they have chosen to create something positive from their pain. They become something more than victims — they become survivors.

Two friends of mine spent a night a week answering calls to

a sexual abuse hot line. Lynda N. Driscoll, who was quoted earlier in this chapter, is the president of Network against Child Abuse, Inc., and a member of the Utah Task Force on Child Sexual Abuse and the Committee on Ritual Abuse. My sister Nancy Anderson devoted much time and effort in helping me with this book in order to regain a sense of power and to affirm her identity as a strong woman working toward a healthy future.

Grief

Grief, like anger, is an emotion many of us have difficulty dealing with. But grief is—or should be—a part of our emotional life. Why? Because it is the normal response to loss, and our lives are full of losses, large and small. Some of the losses we all feel include loss of youth, dreams, abilities, belief in comforting myths (such as the "happily ever after" and the "parents are perfect" myths), opportunities, friendships, confidence, faith, health, loved ones—to mention only a few. Every loss we feel hurts us, and we must allow ourselves to grieve them.

Instead of grieving our losses at the time they occur, we often steel ourselves against hurt by getting on with life, stoically continuing as we were before. But grief, like anger or any other emotion, does not disappear simply because we choose not to acknowledge it. It accumulates. I once described this phenomenon in the following words:

> Mourning has a timetable in the heart
> tears have a schedule all their own
> and when they are deferred
> one must pay interest.
> This I know.
> Behind a dam of ancient griefs ignored
> and little losses never mourned
> my tears back up,
> an ever-growing salty reservoir.

Allowing as much of the hurt and grief as we can at the time we experience a loss is the only way to avoid filling the reservoir to the point of overflowing. But that is only the first step. As with anger, spending some time considering what has caused us to feel hurt is also important. Is it the result of unmet expectation? We need to change our expectation or attempt to change something about the situation. Is it the result of the human condition, such as a loss associated with aging? We need to grieve the loss, but then we need to move on by discovering ways to compensate for it and to maintain our joy in life.

These examples point out the two kinds of things we grieve: those we can do something about and those we can't. Regardless of the category, acknowledging the loss and grief allows us to move through it more quickly. Having the empathetic support of those around us can also play an important part.

Unfortunately, some in the Church have the mistaken notion that if a person grieves a loss — especially the loss of a loved one — it indicates that they are lacking in faith. Such individuals don't really understand the words in Ecclesiastes 3:1 and 4, which tell us: "To every thing there is a season, and a time to every purpose under the heaven: . . . a time to weep, and a time to laugh; a time to mourn, and a time to dance." Because of this attitude, they do not know how to perform one of the important tasks of a baptised member of the Church, to mourn with those who mourn and comfort those who stand in need of comfort. (See Mosiah 18:9; see also chapter 17, "Getting Help/Giving Help.")

In one ward a young man lost his father to a heart attack. The death came without any warning, and the young man was devastated. Every time he tried to express his grief to members of his ward, he was cut off in midsentence with the assurance that his father was in heaven and that he would surely see him again. He wanted to say, "Yes, I know all that. But I *miss* my dad, and it *hurts!*" He had such a difficult time working through his grief in a ward where others denied it that he finally sought solace from friends outside the Church. These friends were willing to allow him to experience his appropriate season of grief.

Victims of abuse — and I include in this category *anyone* who grew up in a dysfunctional family — need to have their appropriate season of grief. They have much to grieve. They grieve for their lost selves, for the child who was never allowed to have a childhood. They weep over lost time, ruined relationships, unrealized potential. They grieve the life that was a lie. Their tears are justified: they have suffered terrible losses. One man struggling with these issues said, "I just feel so sad all the time."

This kind of grieving doesn't usually take place until individuals have to some extent worked through their anger, for sorrow seems to occupy a strata below the anger. In addition, it has its own differing layers, as do all our emotions.

One woman, for example, felt that she had dealt successfully with the dysfunction in her own family. She had faced the fact that her mother had been abusive and her father had been absent. She had even gone so far as to confront her mother. During this time, she experienced a lot of anger and old pain. Her therapy sessions were exhausting: she would come home from them and go directly to bed. But after a time, she felt as though she had gotten through the worst of it.

Several years later, an odd thing began to happen. Every so often, the Negro spiritual "Sometimes I Feel Like a Motherless Child" would pop into her mind. She would be buying groceries or washing dishes, and there the song would be. She felt some sorrow whenever it came to mind, but she thought that was just because the song was sad. She never focused on the feeling long enough to discover the real source.

Then one day, realization broke through. *She* was a motherless child! A wail broke from her lips as another, deeper level of grief opened up.

It was a shattering experience, but grief that is expressed is healthy grief, while (to use the contrast already established) grief that is unacknowledged is toxic grief. However, if a person becomes overwhelmed by their grief and feelings of helplessness and hopelessness, they may need some assistance to move beyond them. We need to walk through the valley of grief, not camp in it.

Forgiveness

Trying to move directly from recognition of past events to forgiveness is not unusual for adult children, either because they do not want to deal with the pain of the other steps or because, as one person said, "I want to get on with my life." Those who attempt it, however, remain vulnerable to the old patterns of dysfunction, for the pressure of unacknowledged feelings and their effects on current relationships will still be strong. Furthermore, complete, long-lasting forgiveness can be given only when a person really knows what needs to be forgiven. The temptation to jump into forgiveness can be great, especially when the victim is encouraged to do so by family, friends, and Church leaders. However, one must first put him- or herself into a position to forgive.

The process that adult children go through as they attempt to resolve the issues relating to dysfunction is rarely understood by those around them. Family and friends see only the pain and the disruption of normal life, and they are often threatened by the emotional roller coaster the adult child is riding. They do not know what to do, but they feel that they must do something.

In an attempt to be helpful, they often say things like, "Why can't you get on with your life?" "You're just hurting yourself by not forgiving." "Can't you just forgive and forget?" "Don't you believe in the Atonement?" "Why can't you let it go?" But as

111

one adult child succinctly put it, "Forgiveness has its own agenda, and intellectual forgiveness is not the goal."

Forgiveness is necessary, of course, but not the kind others might be looking for, the kind that says, "Okay, that's all done. Now we can go on with our lives." *Forgiveness does not mean shoring up the status quo.*

Whom must victims forgive? It may come as a surprise that victims must first forgive themselves — the child or adult they were when the abuse was taking place. What for? For being vulnerable. For being unable to protect themselves. For not shouting "No!" In the case of some victims of long-term sexual abuse, for having had a pleasurable response. This forgiveness of self becomes possible only as adult children learn to put the blame directly where it belongs, *on the abuser.* When they can do that, they no longer condemn themselves for being powerless.

Adult children must also forgive themselves for taking on all kinds of unhealthy behaviors to survive. They begin to do so as they realize that their behaviors were the only way they could cope with what was happening to them at the time. When they can validate the child they were by saying, "You did what you had to. You're a survivor," they feel more able to choose for themselves new, healthy survival techniques.

Must the adult child forgive the abuser? Some professionals say that the healing process can go on without doing so. In fact, making a conscious decision not to immediately forgive can be a way of acknowledging the pain of the self who was abused. It assures the inner child that the horribleness of the act(s) against her has been realized and that her pain will not be ignored again. It assures her that her needs will come before the need of the family to "get back to normal" or the need of the abuser to know that he or she has been forgiven.

Two legitimate needs of the victim may in fact preclude a "normalization" of relationships: the need for safety and the need for justice. If the abuser refuses to admit to the abuse, or admits it but puts the blame on the victim, or will continue it, the victim is justified in choosing to sever the relationship. In less difficult cases, the victim may choose to maintain contact under clearly outlined conditions. Either way, the victim has, as far as possible, made the important step of taking responsibility for his or her safety.

While such choices may disturb family members, the victim's need for justice may lead to an even more disturbing choice: to press charges against the abuser. Physical and sexual abuse are crimes. Initiating appropriate legal action can help the victim get over the feeling of somehow being to blame. It can also restore to the victim a sense of power after years of feeling powerless.

Such actions seem to have little to do with forgiveness. In fact, they may seem to be rather vindictive. However, they can become important aspects of a victim's healing process, and thus they may bring the victim closer to being ultimately able to forgive. Intellectual forgiveness offered as an act of will is not true forgiveness. True forgiveness is a gift of the heart—of the healing, if not healed, heart.

Once Again, with Feeling

In the process of working through powerful and complex emotions, individuals may feel loving and forgiving one day and angry the next. They should not add to their burdens by feeling guilty about an apparent relapse. It is typical of the healing process. Even when adult children reach a plateau of peace in their healing and think, "Wheeew! I'm glad that's over," it probably isn't over.

Actually, the healing process may never be completely over. After many weeks or months of experiencing peace and growth, an incident may occur that brings all of the issues back into the

113

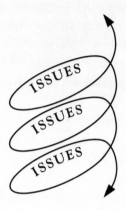

The way we react when confronting problems related to our dysfunctional patterns will either move us upward or downward on the growth spiral.

fore. When that happens, adult children may experience denial, anger, sorrow, and the need to forgive themselves and others all over again.

Will this mean that they have failed in some way? No. All individuals have certain issues that crop up periodically throughout life. Will it mean they are stuck on a treadmill? Not necessarily. Instead of thinking of it as a circle going around and around, one survivor describes it as a spiral going upward. She occasionally experiences the same feelings all over again, but each time she deals with them on a different, higher level and from a position of greater strength. And each time she successfully handles them, she grows even more.

CHAPTER 16

DYSFUNCTION AND SPIRITUAL IDENTITY

As they take the first tentative steps into their inner land-scape, many adult children of dysfunctional families question whether they will find anything inside beyond their rage and grief. They may feel as if nothing is there but a black void. Or, that if something is there, it will be bad or worthless. Their fears are fed by some religious and psychological viewpoints that teach that man is naturally prone to evil and that the rational mind must be in control over the untrustworthy, irrational, emotional subconscious mind.

Belief in the gospel can be a sustaining force and an anchor for those in this situation. For some, however, basic gospel prin-ciples and teachings have been called into question as a result of their experiences. Examining how they feel about these issues can help move the process along.

Our Eternal Identity

Adult children who are Church members may say that all people are children of God, but in actuality they often exclude themselves when they say it. The things that are most basic to their being—individual perception, thoughts, feelings, desires, and choices—have been rejected, denied, or sharply curtailed. First, their parents or other adults have shamed them when they expressed themselves. Over a period of time, they may even have developed a parental voice in their head that continued to shame them. Because they learned to see their inner self as bad and their normal needs as inappropriate, they may have grave doubts about themselves. They fear who they are and what they would become if not controlled, and they have the same fears regarding their spouses and their children.

Those who were abused as children have a specially difficult time feeling good about themselves. They often rationalize their parent's behavior by coming to the conclusion that they deserved abuse because they were bad or they "asked for it."

A fifty-year-old man stood at his parents' graves, tears in his eyes. This man had been the victim of severe abuse all through his childhood until he left home after graduating from high school. A younger brother who had witnessed the abuse noticed the tears and remarked, "How have you managed to forgive Dad for what he did to you?"

The man looked puzzled. "What do I have to forgive him for? I deserved it. I was a slow learner. He did what he had to do to teach me what I needed to know." Thirty-two years after leaving home, this man still believed that something faulty in himself warranted the abuse. He has taken on the responsibility for it, thus absolving his deceased father and allowing his love for his father to remain intact.

Psychologist Virginia Satir makes the assertion that no child is intentionally bad. He is either trying to fill a need in the only way he knows how, responding inappropriately because of poor communication, or acting out his role in the family system. In addition, he may also be suffering from some sort of chemical imbalance or neurological problem. Punishing him for his actions does not promote change; it only teaches him to react violently when he is angry. It also makes him feel devalued.[1]

Having been devalued, adult children conclude that they are guilty or bad. Their shame is so profound, they can't imagine that God would love them or that they are of worth. It may be of some help to adult children to review what scriptures say about who and what we are.

The scriptures tell us our eternal essence is intelligence, or the light of truth. In Doctrine & Covenants 93:29, we read, "Man was also in the beginning with God. Intelligence, or the light of truth, was not created or made, neither indeed can be."

What can neither be created nor made cannot be destroyed. The light of truth remains in an individual—*is* that individual in an eternal sense—regardless of what he does in the course of his evolution. It may be deeply buried, that is true, but it doesn't cease to exist. Therein lies the intrinsic and eternal worth of every soul.

In addition, each individual has been gifted with the light of Christ. John 1:9–10 tells us that "[Christ] was the true Light, which lighteth every man that cometh into the world. He was in the world, . . . and the world knew him not." The fact that the majority of the people on the earth are not aware of the light of Christ within them doesn't change the fact that it is there. Its presence is the reason Christ could also say, "For, behold, the kingdom of God is within you." (Luke 17:21.)

From these scriptures, we can conclude that if we courageously explore those parts of ourselves that we have ignored or even denied, we will encounter a self of eternal worth. Beyond that, we will encounter the light of Christ and the kingdom of God.

Trust in God

Trusting in God can sometimes be difficult even for those of us who have a sense of our eternal identities. Although we know much about the nature of God, our relationship to him is based on faith, and negative images of who and what God is can weaken that faith. Sometimes the image of God as created by the teachings of our parents or other adults has been more threatening than comforting. If that image has persisted into adulthood, it makes us somewhat wary of putting ourselves in his hands.

Those who have (or had) a difficult relationship with their earthly father are also often reluctant to approach God because of the image of God as father. If their earthly father was never pleased, or was abusive or absent, they may fear that their heavenly father is the same. Their fear of being rejected, hurt, or abandonded by God prompts them to create barriers between him and themselves in the misguided belief that those barriers will be a protection.

Trust in a benign God. Women who are or were victims of sexual abuse can have a particularly hard time with this issue because of the anger they feel toward men. They are often angry not only at the abuser, but also at men in general. In addition, if they reported the abuse but nothing was done, they may feel mistrust toward most if not all men in authority.

These feelings can easily carry over into their relationship to God unless they do some work exploring their idea of who God is and can separate him from the men who have hurt them. One victim laughed when her therapist told her, "You don't trust men, not even God." She laughed because she was shocked. She was shocked because it was true. Feeling a great need for some kind of connection with their Heavenly Mother is not unusual for victims, for they see her as accepting and nurturing.

Trust in God's love for us as we are. Adult children often do not believe that God loves them as they are; they believe he will love them only when they have become what he wants them to become. They fear that he will punish them for what they believe are weak, wicked, or unworthy thoughts. And while they often feel angry with God, they fear that if they express their anger, he will either retaliate or be destroyed.

God will not be destroyed by our negative feelings, our doubts, or our poor choices. We do not have to hide them from him—in fact, we cannot hide them from him. When we try, we only succeed in hiding them from ourselves, thus creating blocks to our own progression. God isn't interested in our false, people-pleasing, and God-placating self. On the other hand, when we trust in the unconditional love of God for us *as we are*, we feel free to acknowledge our perceptions, thoughts, feelings, wants, and choices—all of them, whether they are "nice" or not.

This is very important, for putting a lot of energy into repressing negative feelings impairs our ability to feel in general. This includes our ability to feel the burning in the bosom, the peace, the promptings, the comfort, and the love of God for us that the scriptures speak so often of.

In one case, a priesthood holder was burdened with feelings of being angry, used, and hopeless. He dealt with them by boxing them away and "putting his shoulder to the wheel"—doing what he was supposed to do. But his negative feelings were strong, and he had to clamp down hard to keep them from surfacing. In the process, he clamped down on emotions in general. He became unable to experience simple happiness in daily life, to find enjoyment in his activities, or to feel his love for his family and theirs for him. His spirituality suffered as well, for he no longer felt the love of God for him, the sweetness of testimonies borne, or the manifestations of the Spirit in him.

Fear of pain and uncertainty about the outcome keep this man and others in similar situations from doing the very thing that will reconnect them with the feelings that make life worthwhile. When we open ourselves to emotions in general, we also

119

open ourselves to the feelings of joy, love, contentment, and spirituality that we long to experience.

Trust in the mission of Christ. Sadly, many Latter-day Saints who grew up in dysfunctional believe in the Atonement as a principle without believing in it as a power that can change their lives. "That's true for other people but not for me" is often the thought that plagues them. They do not feel that they deserve the love of others, much less the love of Christ as reflected by the Atonement.

In addition, adult children are determinedly self-reliant. They believe that they are responsible for everything, that it is all up to them. They often find it difficult to let go of this attitude and accept the gift that Christ offers to all. When they are able to do so, however, they experience enormous relief, for they finally understand that they do not have to carry their burdens alone.

The 12-step programs, such as those available through Alcoholics Anonymous and Incest Survivors Anonymous, understand both these issues. Participants in them begin by admitting that they are powerless over the difficulties in their lives (alcohol, abuse, perfectionism, chronic illness) and that their lives have become unmanageable. They then work toward developing faith in a "power" greater than themselves, and they turn their lives over to the care of God.

Trust in the principle of agency. Members of unhealthy families have little experience in exercising agency, that is, making a choice based on their own convictions and values. They are often denied experiences that would inform their choices. They are pressured into assuming roles that support the system. They thus have no sense of being able to choose for themselves.

To choose is to exercise power. In the middle of all the uncertainty and turmoil that often accompany change, adult children can begin to make choices about what they want, what they think, what they believe. In order to do so, adult children must learn to ask themselves, "What do I really want?" They must begin to make choices on the basis of what their needs are, not on the expectations of others. For instance, they learn how to say no to a request they are unable or unwilling to comply with. This can be a big step, if as codependents their need to please has often taken precedence over their personal well-being. The ability to make choices is an eternal principle, and it is their right.

And if you can't trust in these things? Often, the only thing adult children trust in is their pain. The pain itself, when it becomes intolerable, is what motivates them to do the work of change. Earnie Larson says, "Recovery starts with enough pain that no matter what it takes, you're willing to get out of the hurt."[2] And, as the saying goes, "The only way out of pain is through it."

If you are at that point, finding a therapist or a group you feel comfortable with and a program that seems valuable to you is important. Then, if you can trust nothing else, trust the program. Trust that doing the work, bit by bit, day after day, will lead to healing, peace, and love.

CHAPTER 17

GETTING HELP/GIVING HELP

Typically, we seek help only when our lives become too painful for us to continue as they are. When we reach that point, there are several avenues through which we can find the support we need. We can

A. Get a referral from our bishop to the local LDS Social Services representative.
B. Talk to our family physician and get a referral from him.
C. Get a referral to a therapist in our HMO. This is not a quick process, but it is often the most affordable.
D. Get the name of a therapist from someone whose opinion we value or from someone who has had a successful experience with therapy.
E. Check with our local hospital concerning program offerings.
F. Attend meetings of one of the 12-step programs. Some of these are Alcoholics Anonymous, Incest Survivors Anonymous, Overeaters Anonymous, Emotions Anonymous, or Adult Children of Dysfunctional Families. Local chapter offices should be listed in the phone book.

Attending a weekly session or group does much to further

the process of dealing with dysfunction and abuse. However, the six days between meetings can be difficult to get through. We also need specific support from our families, friends, and church groups during that time. We often do not know what we need or how to ask for it, though. In addition, our loved ones probably do not know what we need or how to provide it.

The issues surrounding dysfunction, particularly abuse, are complex, and the needs of those who have experienced dysfunction are equally complex. Both adult children and those closest to them need to learn all they can about the subject. The following suggestions offer a starting point from which concerned individuals can move toward understanding the issues.

Check Your Assumptions

All of us—both men and women, both victims and others who are concerned—need to check our assumptions, because the kinds of biases and attitudes that allow abnormal family interaction or violence against the weak are often hidden. We err if we assume that the well-informed and socially enlightened are free of societal biases against either perpetrators or victims. Assuming that the victims themselves are free of such biases and myths is also a mistake. Victims especially need to check their assumptions, since those assumptions may be what is keeping them in abusive situations.

The following questions can serve to increase awareness of our own biases, if honestly answered.

Do you think that

- what happens inside a family's home is nobody's business but their own?
- some things are better left unsaid?
- there is nothing wrong with withholding information from family members?

- withholding financial support or love is a good way to motivate spouse or child to fill expectations?
- withholding needed help can be a good motivational tool?
- withholding physical affection is an appropriate response to anger or disappointment?
- traditional roles of women and men are to be held to without deviation?
- men should carry the entire burden of supporting and guiding their family?
- men who show emotion are weak?
- real men are never needy?
- morality is a matter of black and white with no grey in between?
- you are always right?
- it is more important to be right or justified than it is to express love and extend support?
- children must be made to "toe the line," by strong discipline when necessary?
- children who do not live according to your values should be cut off from contact with the family until they comply?
- emotions get in the way of doing what needs to be done?
- the best way to handle emotions is to ignore them?
- some level of abuse in families can be tolerated as normal?
- violence and abuse would be avoided in families if the spouse and children would do what they're asked to do?
- abuse between siblings is part of growing up?
- verbal and/or physical abuse in the school yard, in neighborhood groups, or even in church groups is something children just have to learn to deal with?
- accusations of abuse must always be handled without going "outside the system" (i.e., the Church)?
- girls who have been sexually abused seduced their abuser in some way ?
- women who are raped asked for it?

• males are rarely victims of sexual abuse?
• boys who have been sexually abused are in danger of developing homosexual tendencies?
• victims of sexual abuse (male or female) need to repent?
• keeping a marriage intact is more important than responding to an accusation of abuse?
• having a temple marriage obligates you to stay with an abusive spouse?
• addressing abuse issues in your family or ward is inapproapriate?
• physical intimacy is a right within marriage, regardless of whether there are difficulties in other areas?
• giving youth appropriate information about their sexuality is dangerous?
• counseling is not necessary to deal with tough family problems?

Do you tend to
• talk to a third person about something that is bothering you rather than to the person involved?
• put others' needs before your own?
• avoid conflict whenever possible by walking away?
• minimize the reality of abuse by using less ugly words like "domestic trouble," "getting physical," and "getting carried away?"
• excuse the abuser's behavior because of everything he or she has to deal with?

You may have experienced a strong reaction when reading these questions. You may have become angry or felt great grief. You may have felt some of the questions were inappropriate. Whatever your response, please take the time to honestly assess your answers to these questions. They may serve to indicate areas in which you hold to some myths about abuse or some beliefs about parenting and relationships that can result in abusive behavior or in tolerating abusive behavior toward oneself or others.

125

For some, they may have made the dysfunctional or abusive nature of a current relationship clear. If that is true in your case, you may wish to turn to the appendix, "What Next?"

The rise in abuse cases throughout the country will continue unless each of us roots out of our thought patterns assumptions that perpetuate myths about abuse. As it was put in one of the abuse sessions at the 1990 BYU Women's Conference, when we perpetuate myths about abuse, we become perpetrators.

The next two sections of this chapter deal specifically with the needs of abuse victims. They address the extreme manifestation of dysfunction. By the time individuals finally seek help, the abuse they have been experiencing—perhaps for years—has escalated to the point that they can no longer tolerate it. Their need for appropriate help is urgent.

Because of the dramatic rise in abuse cases, we cannot discount the possibility that we ourselves, someone in our extended family, or someone in our circle of friends may either become victims or may be approached by a victim for help. Would we know what to do if that were the case? Would our reactions really help, or would they add to the pain of the victim? The following guidelines indicate some of the issues we may very well have to deal with.

Suggestions on Helping Victims

Believe the victim's words. This is particularly important, since it takes enormous courage for a victim to speak out after long years of silence. If their story is discounted or disbelieved, they typically retreat back into silence. Months or years may pass before they gain the courage to again speak the truth.

The fact is that few people want to believe victims. Accepting their story as truth is too painful, so listeners often find their own way to make it less horrible. Some discount what they hear. "Jane," who told her story in the *Exponent II* issue on abuse, related that some in whom she confided dismissed what she told them by saying she was overly emotional and dramatic.[1]

Others attempt to make the abuse seem less awful by not using the strong words that express exactly what it is. But rape is rape, not something else. Battering is battering, not "getting a little physical."

Do some who cry "Abuse!" lie? Some. But only some. And even trained therapists and counselors are not always able to make a judgment call with complete confidence in such cases. One doctor with experience in the field says having a "willing suspension of disbelief" when women or children report sexual abuse is critical. Judy Dushku summarizes the doctor's position in this way:

> After many years of wrestling with this [issue], he felt that it was most appropriate to lean towards accepting the stories of the women and children. Why? He explained that it was because of the far greater potential for life-long damaging and scarring that comes from a victim daring to report abuse and not being believed. Many children who are abused try only once to tell their story. If they are not believed, they retreat into guilt and self-destructive modes that often never heal. They never regain the courage or positive self-image to try again. When this happens, there is very little hope for later healing. Because not being believed at that crucial time is so critical, the risk of an error in judgment being made is too great. So although admitting the wrong choice can hurt an innocent father, this doctor had decided that he would believe a woman or child accusing a husband/father of incest or other sexual abuse.[2]

Gain understanding. Common sense does not go very far in understanding the dynamics of what is happening in an abusive relationship, the effects of abuse on the victim and other family members, and the process the victim needs to go through to regain a healthy sense of personhood.

The importance of informing yourself cannot be overstressed, whether you are the victim or a family member. In either case, you have a lot of issues that will, sooner or later, come to the surface and demand attention. You will find that asking for or offering appropriate support is much easier if you understand the feelings and behaviors inherent in the process.

If you are a family member, you will need to begin your own process because you undoubtedly have issues of your own to deal with. (Remember how dysfunction affects the whole family unit, generation after generation.) Sometimes the very best gift you can give to a victim—and to yourself—is to do your own emotional work.

Allow everyone the time they need. Dealing with abuse issues takes time, a lot of it. Don't rush the process. If you are the victim, gently and lovingly allow yourself the time you need to work through the difficult emotions you are experiencing. If you are a concerned friend or family member, respect the victim's need for time. Don't pressure them by asking well-meaning but tactless questions such as, "Aren't you getting over this yet? How come it's taking so long?"

Remember also that even when all concerned feel they are ready to go forward again, events can trigger a whole new round of pain, anger, and grief. Trying to put these emotions out of mind does not make them go away. Acknowledge that they need to be recognized and dealt with perhaps many times, so that the victim can minimize feelings of anger and guilt at having to go through it all over again.

Offer your simple presence. If an abuse victim trusts you enough to reveal his or her circumstances to you, don't give in to the temptation to try to solve everything or to be a caretaker—a codependent. Victims are not asking you to "make it better."

128

You can't. Even those in helping organizations can't "make it better." The most they can do is intervene when necessary and support as needed. Therefore, your simple presence is the greatest gift you can give a victim.

It is not easy to listen to someone in pain without feeling as though you have to make some response or identify with the pain. You may be flooded with strong emotions, especially if you are a victim yourself. Don't allow your emotions to get out of proportion. Remember your boundaries: You are not the victim in this case.

There are incidents, however, when individuals first recognize that they were abused when they hear someone else's story. In such cases, emotions in response to the story are very strong and frightening.

If you feel a great deal of anger at what you are hearing, use it constructively. For instance, become an advocate for victims. Take training and volunteer to man a hot line. Inform yourself and teach others what you have learned.

However, if you find that you are becoming overwhelmed emotionally or reacting in a codependent manner, it may be appropriate for you to help the victim find another support person. Explain that you love and care for him or her, but that your own situation requires giving support in a way that is healthy for you both.

When Priesthood Authority Is Involved

Victims of abuse who turn to priesthood authority for help have special needs. Because telling their story to those in authority can be difficult, they approach a meeting with their bishop or stake president with anxiety. Often they have wavered for a considerable time before gaining enough courage to even make the appointment.

Talking about their problems is particularly difficult for

women who are being abused by their husbands, especially if those husbands are priesthood holders who have callings of some significance in the Church hierarchy. Recognizing this difficulty, some leaders have found it helpful to designate a woman as liaison between themselves and the victims. Having a woman liaison allows victims to speak openly to someone with whom they feel more comfortable.

When abuse victims seek priesthood guidance, they do so with the fervent prayer that something will be done to alter their situation. Their worst fear is that the response will be, "He's a good man (or woman). He (or she) may be having some difficulties right now. Let's hold on and see what happens." The real danger in such situations is that the victims might return to a situation in which they are at risk.

In addition, victims of every age and either sex are in great need of having their self-worth reaffirmed. They need to know that regardless of what has happened to them, their Father in Heaven has not ceased to love them. Victims of sexual abuse in particular need the reassurance that they are "still clean in the eyes of God and others."[3]

When someone in a family is abusive, the whole family needs help. A bishop who is aware of appropriate services available through Church agencies — as well as city and county agencies — can refer both the victim and other family members to helping organizations.

Some situations are beyond that relatively simple solution, however. Assault is a crime. Although legal action may be distasteful to all involved, there are times when it is the most appropriate response. Women who have taken legal steps often feel that other ward members look upon them with disapproval, which the members express through insensitive comments, in lack of understanding, or in lack of loving support.

The attitude of priesthood authorities in such instances can

130

be influential in creating and maintaining the necessary climate of support. But while the priesthood has a significant role to play in helping dysfunctional families, the severity of the problem is such that all members must do what is necessary to increase their awareness.

CHAPTER 18

HEALING: THE TASK OF LIFE

During our earthly life, we are separated to one extent or another from our eternal nature by the veil. We are also separated from our brothers and sisters, not being of one mind and one heart, and we are separated from our Father in Heaven. Overcoming these separations is our prime task; helping others overcome them is our mission. Regardless of the shape our individual lives take, the task and mission at the core is the same.

We cannot make significant progress in this direction unless we attend to the wounds of a dysfunctional childhood or a dysfunctional relationship. We have hidden behind a barrier intended to protect us from hurt, only to discover that it contributes to the perpetuation of the separation. The false self, as has been noted, is yet another layer removed from our true spiritual identity. (See charts, pages 51, 72.) We are never able to connect with others meaningfully until we begin to connect with our true selves.

Recognizing our woundedness and taking the steps toward healing that are within our power form the essence of what we are called to do. When we begin to heal, we become more sensitive to things spiritual. We feel an inner need to communicate with our Savior and our Father. We feel the change of heart spoken of in the scriptures. We then are in a position to take advantage of the Atonement, the greater healing that was the mission of the Savior.

As we are healed, the Spirit's influence moves us to reach out with healing hands to others. The change we feel in ourselves is felt by them. One by one, changed lives change other lives. This transformation is what lies at the core of the gospel: we become new creatures.

New Ways of Knowing

Although scripture has many stories of individuals who undergo this change as the result of one dramatic experience, for most of us the change comes slowly. And it begins with a shift not only in what we think — but also in the way we think. The healing activities suggested in a wide range of popular medical and psychological literature involve quite different mental processes than many people are used to working with. These ways of thinking and knowing are associated with right-brain activity.

Left-brain thinking is sequential, analytical, rational, objective, literal, and detail oriented. The scientific method, based on left-brain thinking, is the accepted way of arriving at truth. We measure, weigh, take apart, and record tangible features. We come to conclusions through logic. Our culture validates, encourages, and teaches this type of thinking.

Right-brain thinking, on the other hand, is simultaneous and visual; that is, we might "see" or understand the whole of a concept at once. It searches for patterns and seeks an overview rather than focusing on details. It is synthetical, meaning that it connects elements together rather than examines them separately or even takes them apart. It is intuitive: it makes "leaps of faith," "jumps to conclusions," and arrives at understanding without benefit of logic. It is subjective, based on the way an individual feels about something—knowing through feelings. In addition, through the right brain we gain access to ideas and information from the vast subconscious, that part of us we rarely make deliberate effort to access.

Children utilize their right-brain functions when they are young. They learn by seeing and hearing, not by reading, applying logic, or analyzing. They trust their instincts. They are open to intuition. They relish creative activities and are unconcerned with how the results are received.

Then they start school, where they learn over the years that only certain ways of doing things or seeing things are valid. They are taught that logic and the scientific method form the basis for human progress, that subjective opinion is only valid in certain limited areas, and that a whole can be best understood by analyzing its parts. They are rarely taught the two ways of thinking, the circumstances in which each is most appropriately used, and the skill of alternating between them in a complementary manner.

It isn't surprising, then, that both our education system and popular wisdom reject the validity of subjective response. For example, an art critic might deride the statement, "I don't know much about art, but I know what I like," even though art evaluation is partly subjective. Actually, because an individual's subjective response is honest, it is also valid regardless of how uneducated it may be.

Dysfunctional families also reject the validity of subjective response. Children in such families frequently learn to keep their opinions to themselves, the same way they learn to keep their feelings hidden. They do so because the adults in their lives are controlling and critical.

Children internalize the parental voices they hear. It is important that they do so, for in their early years those voices exercise a controlling and protecting influence. The parental

134

voices children from healthy families internalize are nurturing and affirming as well as critical. The voices adult children have internalized are almost exclusively critical.

Adult children thus end up with particularly harsh internal critics and editors. These critics and editors are enemies of the right brain. Under the influence of internal censure, adult children reject impulses, intuition, or creative thoughts, often automatically. They may reject them so quickly that they may not even be aware of them, for the right brain is nonaggressive and does not persist in the face of rejection.

Adult children may also consciously reject the thoughts originating in the right brain because they do not trust them. Such thoughts lie outside the rational, controlled ways of thinking and experiencing the world, and adult children spend much of their lives controlling themselves and others. Doing otherwise thus goes against the grain. Once such ways of thinking and feeling are accepted, however, right-brain ways of knowing can be used to reestablish communication with our inner selves.

The Divided Self

As mentioned, the right brain is the link between our conscious and subconscious minds. It is also the link between our egos and the part of self that is eternal, that lived with a heavenly being in the premortal life. Writers who work with adult children refer to different levels of self, such as the *inner child, wise one, inner guide,* or *higher parent.* I am aware that these terms may sound like "psychobabble" to some, but it is possible to fit them into a gospel context.

The inner child. The inner child can be thought of as that innocent self that came directly from the presence of God. Living with repressive parenting rules, stressors, and shame caused her to retreat for protection behind a false front. But she is still there,

135

and the tender, immediate knowledge she had of her Heavenly Father is still intact.

The inner-child aspect of our nature has the capacity for unconditional love. She also has the capacity for spontaneity, a willingness to risk, the courage to try and try again. She is the keeper of the sense of humor. She has an open connection to the creative urge.

If the emotional and growth needs of the inner child were not met, she has been blocked in her development. She has become needy, hurt, and hungry. She feels threatened when events occur similar to painful situations of the past. She does not trust people. She perceives the world as a scary, unsafe place.

We don't get the benefit of the positive aspects of the inner child if she is still wounded. If we do try to make connection without addressing her issues, she will object, rather strenuously. There is no child that can throw a tantrum like the neglected inner child. On the other hand, there is no child that can bring joy into our lives like the inner child, if we protect and nurture her.

The higher parent. As has been mentioned, the parental voice internalized by children of dysfunctional families is very critical, more often destructive than nurturing. In addition, few of us were parented the way we wanted to be. As part of healing, we seek the love and affirmation we missed and still yearn for. We seek them from others, but the most important and reliable source is within, our higher parent.

Visualizing the higher parent is a way of personalizing the part of our adult self that is capable of unconditional love. Our inner parent can profoundly fill the emotional needs of both our adult self and our inner child, for he knows far more about what is required and the best way to provide it. In fact, with the exception of our heavenly parents, our inner parent is the most reliable source of nurturance available to us, if we consistently take the time to connect with him.

The inner guide or wise one. Most people have had the experience of suddenly knowing the solution to some problem or the decision that must be made in a difficult situation. They refer to such incidents as hunches or intuition. Wise one or inner guide refer to the part of self from which such knowledge comes. They describe our spirit consciousness, which still remembers the truths learned in the premortal existence and which has access to what might be termed universal knowledge.

When we work at establishing a connection with our inner guide, we are actively and directly seeking knowledge that comes through alternate ways of knowing, such as intuition, ways of knowing more valid in some circumstances than logic or scientific method.

Luke 17:21 tells us, "The kingdom of God is within you." That is a difficult concept for many people to grasp since they rarely take time to be aware of what is going on in the various levels of their inner selves. But the words are not merely a figure of speech. They reflect an important spiritual reality. The aspects of our nature described in this section are part of that spiritual reality. Taking the time to know them, and thereby ourselves, well and truly is not an indulgence; it is part of the path by which we enter that kingdom.

CHAPTER 19

THE FOUR RS

The four steps in the healing process we've talked about so far give a good general idea of the basic elements in each person's search for wholeness. To review, they are (1) facing the facts about our childhood, (2) feeling the feelings we have denied, in some cases for years, (3) dealing with the issue of forgiveness as is appropriate to the situation, and (4) learning how to get and give appropriate help.

These first steps, as has been mentioned, are not completed in a one-time effort. As events in our present life bring up issues of the past, we find it necessary to go through them again. This is to be expected and is not a detriment to the process as a whole.

However, some adult children become stuck on this level. They find some payoff in treading the same ground over and over. Perhaps they become addicted to the heightened emotions. Perhaps they fear the kind of substantial change required in the next steps. Whatever the reasons, some do not make real progress despite attending groups, getting therapy, and reading numerous books. They become intellectually knowledgeable about dysfunction without doing the emotional work. As a phrase commonly used in 12-step programs puts it: They talk the talk, but they don't walk the walk.

One way to ensure that we do not get stuck is to do some of the activities designed to change our thought and behavior patterns. They fall into categories I call the four Rs: reconnecting, reparenting, releasing, and restructuring.

What follows is an introduction to these concepts and the kinds of tasks leading to change that are typical of each. You may choose to do some of the activities as they are described here. Or you may use the information in searching out classes, groups, or books that work with a specific area in depth.

Reconnecting

Reconnecting with our divided selves is accomplished through a variety of right-brain activities such as visualization and journal-writing.

Visualization. Visualization is the process by which we allow images from our right brain or our subconscious into our conscious minds. Typically, we begin with a relaxation technique, which puts us in a calm and receptive frame of mind. We then move on to the visualization itself, which in this instance is designed to support the goal of reconnecting. We might visualize our inner child, for example, and carry on a conversation with her. We might ask her what she needs from us and offer her the comfort she has been longing for. If we need guidance in some area, we might visualize our higher parent and ask for advice.

This inner dialogue is quite different from the normal conversations we have with ourselves on a daily basis. The images and information we receive in this process come from our subconscious, which is a vast storehouse of information we are not consciously aware of. In addition, listening to and relying on the inner self (as in meditation or prayer) also seems to be a part of connecting with the Spirit, and thus gives us access to the source of universal truth. For these reasons, directions that we receive

139

in this manner are quite different from the conclusions we might arrive at using a rational thought process.

Journal writing. The kind of journal one writes as a reconnecting activity is not the kind that becomes a part of family history. It is a private, as opposed to a public, journal — what one journal-writer refers to as a "burn-at-my-death" journal, in which anything and everything goes. The kind of journal-writing we do in such a book is therefore quite cathartic. By putting our feelings into words we not only understand them better, we can more easily let go of them.

If a piece of blank paper is intimidating, you might want to try timed writing. Set your kitchen timer for five minutes and write until it rings. Once you start, don't stop no matter how clumsy your words seem to you. Rarely does a session end without some positive effect. If you need to have a starting point, give yourself a topic such as your earliest memories or emotionally significant events relating to one of your particular issues.

Reparenting

Reparenting activities are designed to give us what we wanted from our parents but didn't get. As part of growing up and healing, we learn to provide for ourselves what we need, rather than wait for someone else to provide it for us.

Affirmations. Affirmations are a powerful way to reparent. Adult children may never have heard parental statements that affirmed their worth, such as "I like you," "I'm glad you're here," "You're nice to be around," "You have a place in this home." Statements like these tell us that we are worthy of love and respect just because we are human beings. When we say something affirmative, we give that message to the inner child, who is hungry to hear them.

We can make affirmations in several different ways. They are particularly powerful when combined with visualization, for then we connect a visual image with the positive statement. For example, the affirmation "I am lovable and loving" may be thought or spoken while imagining ourselves responding to a situation in a lovable and loving way. Visualizing an affirming event we always wished had happened, such as hearing a parent say, "I love you," is also powerful.

Affirmations can be written as well. For example, we can write our own bill of rights, including such statements as "I have the right to be happy" and "I have the right to make mistakes." Or we can affirm our worth by writing ourselves permission slips allowing us to have fun and enjoy life, even though we aren't perfect: "I, Carroll Morris, give myself permission to play, even if the wash isn't caught up."

Sometimes we may get frustrated or even angry that we have to do these things for ourselves. We wish that someone else would notice our needs and take care of us! But continuing to hope that others—parents, spouses, or even children—will do so is a sad waste of time, especially for adult children whose parents may never have dealt with the dysfunction in the family. The fact is, no one, not even the best parents, can fill all our emotional needs. Coming to grips with that fact is sad. We grieve over the loss of the myth that others can make us happy. But recognizing the loss, processing it, and moving on to take care of ourselves are major aspects of healing.

Self-care. Most of us don't really know what nurturing ourselves means. Some of us confuse nurturing with self-indulgence. Indulgence makes us feel good for the moment. Nurture makes us feel good on a deeper and more enduring level. For example, a man who snuggles under the covers for another five minutes when he is already late for an important appointment isn't nurturing himself, he's indulging himself. A more appropriate response would be for him to get up early so he could eat a good breakfast, get dressed without rushing, and arrive at work with

141

time enough to prepare mentally for the meeting ahead. The latter choice would reflect appropriate self-care.

While some of us confuse self-indulgence with nurturing, others believe that self-care is indulgence. They believe that taking a nap when they are tired is indulgence, that taking the time to exercise, read, play, or pursue a favorite hobby is indulgence. They thus deny themselves the sort of activities that are enriching.

In the process of reparenting, we learn to nurture and care for the tender, vulnerable self within. We respond to the needs of the inner child for comfort and reassurance, play, spontaneity, excitement, and humor. As part of our healing, we learn to laugh again. We also learn to better recognize and take care of our physical needs.

Releasing

An important part of changing the way we think about things is learning to let go of attitudes and behaviors that create barriers between us and others. That process is called releasing.

A critical step toward releasing is learning to think about our expectations differently. Expectations are the shoulds and oughts from our list that we project upon others. They are the things we think we must do and others must do for us to feel okay. For example, a person might expect that his or her children must be smart, thin, popular and that they should serve missions. The spouse must be good-looking, successful, and well-thought-of. The lawn must be green, the house, clean. If we learn to think of these and other must-haves as *preferences*, we find it easier to let go of perfectionistic standards that may be making us and our loved ones unhappy.

As we begin letting go of expectations, we find it easier to release other attitudes and behaviors, such as judging, fixing, controlling, and manipulating. However, since much of our parenting may be based on these attitudes and behaviors, we may at first feel that we are abdicating our role as parents. That is not the case, however. We do not cease loving and supporting those around us when we let go. Rather, we cease trying to fix them—to solve all their problems the way *we* think they should be solved.

Remembering the popular Serenity Prayer can help us let go of things that are not in our power to change: "Lord, grant me the serenity to accept the things I cannot change, the courage to change the things I can, and the wisdom to know the difference."

Restructuring

Once we have done some work with reconnecting, reparenting, and releasing, we begin to sense the need for a new structure of thought and action that supports the work we have already accomplished. In restructuring, we examine our old speech and thought patterns, then work toward replacing them with new, more appropriate speech and thought patterns. The process includes some of the following points (these are popular topics in continuing-education classes, personal-growth seminars, and self-help books):

> *Clarifying values:* Deciding what things are important to us, what we want out of life and in our relationships.
>
> *Creating proper boundaries:* Learning to differentiate between our opinions, feelings, and problems and the opinions, feelings, and problems that really belong to others.
>
> *Changing the way we talk to others:* Learning appropriate ways of communicating what we think, feel, and want. Learning how to say no.
>
> *Changing the way we talk to ourselves:* Learning how to combat

143

negative self-talk. Restructuring our thoughts in more positive patterns.

Doing any of these restructuring activities is impossible without developing a life-style based on awareness. We need to become more aware of what we are feeling and thinking at any given moment; we need to be more aware of the result we want out of a situation. Only then can we make appropriate decisions on how to act.

The process of becoming aware of what we do and why we do it is a process of spiritual growth. Unconscious patterns (natural-man responses) are a block to spirituality. The more we become aware of our negative thoughts and behavior patterns, the more we become able to choose actions that are Christlike.

CHAPTER 20

CREATING A DAILY PROGRAM

Once adult children have worked through some of the emotional issues of dysfunction and taken steps toward reconnection, reparenting, releasing, and restructuring, they often feel ready to move on with their lives. They know that they aren't really finished with those issues, but they have gained some measure of peace. They want to reenter the flow of normal life and progress from healing to growth.

Adult children find that devising and working some sort of daily program helps keep them clear and current as they move back into life. This is critical if they are to avoid falling into the patterns from the past that enslaved them. The daily program can either be one they have devised themselves, incorporating what they have learned about dysfunction and the needs of adult children, or it can be one adopted from a helping organization such as a 12-step group.

It is important to note that following a daily program is different from "doing the checklist," because the program has been *chosen*, not imposed. And the elements are supportive of the individual's desire for growth, not the system's desire for status quo.

Unfortunately, the kinds of daily programs that many Church members struggling with dysfunction create for themselves often focus on increased activity as a way of dealing with personal pain. They rely on will power and rigid control to solve problems or to deal with compulsive/addictive behavior. Sometimes well-meaning local leaders reinforce this tendency. Lacking an understanding of the complexities of dysfunction, they have counseled those in pain to go home, read their scriptures, say their prayers, try to love their spouse, and serve someone else more needy. While every one of those suggestions has value, they do not address the issues that cause dysfunction.

A personal program designed to keep us moving in the right direction will include activities supporting each of the following issues of adult children:

- living in the now
- increasing spirituality
- providing self-care
- dealing with addictive/compulsive behavior
- improving our relationships

Living in the Now

How many of us spend our lives living either in the future or in the past? We either worry about what may happen or we agonize over what has happened. In either case, we replay a scenario over and over, concocting alternate versions. We can get so caught up in this that we lose sight of the only part of our life that is real, and that is *this moment.*

Living in the now requires that we be honest about what we think, feel, and want and that we allow others to be honest also. Living in the now means that we focus on *what is,* not *what if.* We cease blaming others for our actions or emotions and take

146

responsibility for our choices. By doing so, we set down the burden of past events and the desire for future recompence or retribution.

When we live in the now, we do not put off repentance or forgiveness, for we understand that there is only one proper time for them: this very moment. Guilt and the desire for revenge are thus not carried over from one moment into the next. I have the feeling that those who are aware, who are focused and committed enough to repent and forgive in the second that sin or insult occurs, come as close to achieving perfection in this life as possible.

Meditation is a practice that helps us to live in the now by teaching us how to keep our thoughts focused. Meditation is simple yet hard. One effective approach is to begin by sitting in a comfortable posture and consciously quieting your body. Focus on the rhythm of your breathing. Observe the activities of your mind. It can be a real education! You'll be amazed at the range of things your mind will come up with. Some will have to do with your tasks of the day or your plans for the week. Others will be tied into what is happening in your relationships. Still others will be old, old companions, thoughts that have been with you off and on for many years. Such thoughts will keep you engaged on the natural-man level. When you are feeling fearful, worried, guilty, or ashamed, there is no room in your consciousness for anything else.

Your first impulse as you watch your thoughts will probably be to change them in some way. That is not necessary. All that is necessary is to be aware of your thoughts, to acknowledge them—and then let them pass by without investing any energy into them. Others will follow in an unending parade. In fact, it has been said that "meditation is just one insult after another."

There is one caution for abuse victims, however. The thoughts or pictures coming into your mind may concern events that you are incapable of dealing with on your own. If they

147

become too disturbing, you can stop the process by bringing yourself back to the present and opening your eyes.

Meditation gives us a clear understanding of the working of our minds. It allows us to acknowledge the issues we have held onto for years. It gives us the chance to observe dispassionately — and then let go. In addition, meditation strengthens our ability to be a detached witness or observer, which will help us to maintain a neutral stance in the middle of a family drama or during other negative patterns of behavior.

Increasing Spirituality

Meditation can also help us increase our spirituality. When we meditate regularly, the mind becomes quiet. We are then in a state conducive to receiving the promptings of the Holy Spirit. In fact, meditating regularly can be viewed as evidence of our desire for spiritual experiences, because by doing so, we invite them into our lives.

President David O. McKay wrote, "Meditation is one of the most secret, most sacred doors through which we pass into the presence of the Lord."[1] Church programs tend to emphasize the practical, rational aspects of the gospel rather than the mystical and contemplative aspects. Thus, it is critical for members to have some sort of daily practice that will encourage them, as the Lord said, to "be still and know that I am God" (D&C 101:16). In the quiet space created by consistent meditation, tapping into our essential selves, our eternal selves is possible. Coming closer to the light of Christ within us is also possible. Meditation indicates our desire for spiritual experiences by making a place for them in our lives.

Much of the work of developing and increasing spirituality rests with the individual. Each must put forth effort to read scriptures, pray, fast, and serve. However, the organization of the Church provides important support. For example, one of the primary purposes of attending sacrament meeting is to worship the Father and the Son. Sunday School classes cover the Standard Works each four years, giving us the opportunity to read, ponder, and discuss the scriptures. Fast-and-testimony meetings provide an opportunity to draw nearer to the Spirit, to help those in need, and to express our gratitude to our Heavenly Father. More importantly, the organized Church gives us access to priesthood blessings and gospel ordinances.

It should be mentioned that this approach to church activity differs substantively from the perfectionistic, checklist-oriented approach. In this case, the Church and its programs are seen as means, not as ends in themselves. Activity in the Church is then our aid to growth, not (as it can be) a way of being so busy that the real issues don't have to be faced.

Balance is the key. The structure and support offered by the Church is important, and we need to take advantage of them. But they can't take the place of the inner, solitary work of developing spirituality.

Providing the Nurture and Self-care We Need

Our daily program needs to include taking some time for ourselves — and the first thing we need to do during that time is *discover what we need!* Do we feel tired? We need to rest. Do we feel lonely? We need someone to give us a hug. Do we feel that people are taking advantage of us? We need to state our feelings clearly and indicate what we would like to see happen. Whether our needs are physical, emotional, or spiritual, awareness is the first step toward getting them filled.

Some of our needs we can fill ourselves. We are the only ones who can make sure we eat properly and get enough exercise and sleep. We are the only ones who can say no when we are feeling overwhelmed. We are the only ones who can make sure we have proper medical and dental care.

But there are other needs that are associated with relationships. In those cases, it is up to us to express those needs clearly and tell the person involved how we would like him or her to respond. This is true whether the situation involves a family member, a coworker, or our Church calling. Our needs often go unmet when we expect those around us to guess at what they are. They may still go unmet—but we have no control over that. All we have control over is our own response to our own needs.

My husband, Gary, and I have our wedding anniversary in late May. Since it is typically an extremely busy time of year for us, there have been many times when we could not do much more to celebrate than exchange cards and have a nice meal together. As our twentieth anniversary approached, however, I realized that I wanted a special celebration. I dropped a few hints to Gary, but I had no idea whether he would act on them. Then one afternoon I went for a walk with a good friend of mine. Our whole time together was spent discussing the fiasco of her wedding anniversary, which had recently come and gone. I realized then that if I was really serious about wanting to observe our anniversary with some special activity, I would have to express my expectations clearly rather than hinting and hoping! The result was a lovely occasion that we both remember fondly.

Taking care of ourselves shows that we *care* for ourselves. A clear signal that we have slipped into feelings of worthlessness or have reverted to codependence is behavior that runs counter to our own well-being. In that case, we may need to get back in touch with ourselves by reprocessing some of the issues we discovered when working with the 4 Rs.

We not only need to take care of the adult self, we need to make sure the inner child is receiving the nurturing she needs. Moving on with our lives does not mean that we give her a pat on the head and send her to play in the sandbox by herself. We need to go play with her. In fact, maintaining connection with the inner child is absolutely critical. If we do the work of re-connecting, only to turn our backs on that part of self, we will be back to where we started. Actually, we will be in a worse position, for our inner child will not trust us when we make overtures again.

Remaining open, current, and clear when our inner child is angry is impossible, and making connections with our spiritual self when she is demanding attention is also difficult. When we nurture ourselves, that is, when we take time to do things we deeply enjoy or that satisfy some of our needs, we also nourish the inner child.

Dealing with Addictive/Compulsive Behavior

Most of us from dysfunctional families have some sort of compulsive or addictive behaviors. As part of a program for getting and staying healthy, we need to make a commitment to managing or eliminating our addiction. This requires that we be honest about what it is, especially if it is an "acceptable" addiction such as working, jogging, reading, or fixing.

The cycle of indulgence leads to shame, which leads to more indulgence. In the case of substance abuse or compulsive behavior, a commitment to abstinence helps to break that cycle. Of course, it isn't as easy as saying, "I'm not going to do that anymore." If it were, no one would have a problem with addictions. In addition, abstinence is not necessarily the solution when one is addicted to something that is destructive only when carried to extremes or done compulsively, such as eating or exercising.

The kind of support offered by group therapy or a 12-step program is indispensable. Kicking an addiction is generally not a do-it-yourself project. 12-step programs help in other ways beyond directly addressing the addictive behavior. They address many codependency issues and help participants develop trust in

God. One LDS woman remarked, "I go to my 12-step meeting to be spiritually fed."

Improving Our Relationships

The relationship issues of adult children do not go away. We must keep working with the issues that have kept us from being truly intimate. That means we continue to be aware of the fears and ghosts from the past that inhibit us.

Improving our relationships with others. It is vital that we continue to be clear about what feels good to us, what we need, and what we won't accept in terms of behavior from others who are important to us, whether family member, sweetheart, or friend. In addition, we need to invest the time and energy necessary into maintaining relationships. Two ways of doing that are being present for others when they need us and asking forgiveness of them when appropriate.

Improving ourselves. We can improve our skills in areas of interest. We can use our imagination to stretch our minds. We can take nonthreatening risks and try something new.

Reaching out to others. As we begin to heal, we realize what a wonderful gift has been granted us. Our desire to reach out to others, to serve them in whatever way we can increases. Reaching out is a way for victims of physical and sexual abuse to empower themselves. They can take a stance against abuse in their personal life, speak to groups on abuse, man hot lines, or help other victims go through the grief stages that they themselves have experienced. They thus encourage the healing of others who are wounded.

However, it bears reiterating that we must also be aware of our limitations. If we feel ourselves being drawn into a co-dependent relationship or if some of our own issues are resurfacing strongly, it is a good idea to help the individual find another "buddy" or support person.

Having a daily program helps us to keep current, to keep our emotional pathways unclogged and our spirits unburdened. It keeps us focused on the tasks that help us maintain balance. It moves us forward by encouraging us to engage in growth-promoting activities. If we slacken or feel ourselves slipping, we know what to do, because we have learned during our healing process what works for us. And if a particular part of our program stops working for any reason, we change it by finding new activities that support our interests and goals. It is, after all, our program.

CHAPTER 21

FOLLOWING THE VISION

Chapter one of this book begins with the words, "Nothing is so painful as realizing the gap between what can be and what is. That realization is especially painful in regard to family life." It is especially painful because much of what gives our lives meaning is bound up in relationships, family relationships in particular. We yearn and strive for the sweetness that unconditional love and peace offer. But many of us have not been entirely successful in our efforts.

The changes that we long for come as we confront beliefs and attitudes that have kept us stuck in negative, destructive behaviors and as we work at changing them. We find, however, that change does not come all at once: We take one step forward and two back; we fail, but we try again. In the process we learn ways of relating that bring more positive results.

What keeps us going when we're not making the kind of progress we wish for? A clear vision of what we really want in our lives and in our relationships. In his "Making Things Happen" seminars, therapist Roger Allen encourages participants to find their own inner vision and make a commitment to live by it.[1] Held to over time, a true commitment to such an inner vision becomes more compelling than past patterns and justifications.

154

Inner vision has the power to help us change our attitudes and behaviors because it comes from that part of us sensitive to things of the Spirit. Our longings are always for something better, our struggle is always upward. Even when we experience contentment, enjoyment, and everyday happiness, we sense that there is yet something more. An impulse inherent in our natures as children of God prompts us to reach upward even beyond happiness to joy — the kind of joy that is spoken of in the scriptures, the kind that comes when we fulfill the nature of our being, which is godliness.

Those moments when we are able to transcend our past patterns and act from love give us a taste of that joy. They reinforce our vision and imbue us with the strength to continue our quest.

And it is of utmost importance that we do continue, for the work we do will have an effect not only on us personally, but also on our families now, in the future, and in the eternities. Viewed this way, the work of healing dysfunctional relationships is clearly and essentially a spiritual endeavor. More than that, it is a spiritual necessity. The gospel of Jesus Christ and the principles of family relationships point in the same direction. They are not in conflict with each other.

In spite of that fact, some turn away from the Church in their search for healing. They have been so wounded by certain member teachings and LDS societal pre- and proscriptions, or they have so little faith that the gospel can help them heal, that they no longer feel able to continue as active members. This is unfortunate, for the gospel gives us a strong and sure foundation upon which to stand while we make the first uncertain forays in the direction of healing. At a time when we are forced to examine and question many aspects of our lives, it provides a much-needed anchor.

155

Gospel-based Principles of Relationships

From the scriptures we know that the highest principles governing relationships are eternal worth, the freedom to choose, and the power of love to influence for good. These principles also govern healing. Although they have been discussed previously, they are important enough to merit a short restatement here.

Eternal worth. Intelligence, the very stuff that forms our essence, cannot be created or made. It is coeternal with God (see D&C 93:29). It is light and truth. It is, in fact, the glory of God (see D&C 93:36). We then, in our pure state, contribute to God's glory. No wonder he enjoins us to "Remember the worth of souls is great in the sight of God" (D&C 18:10).

Eternal worth thus springs not from accomplishment, but from being, from our very essence as eternal entities. This knowledge forms the bedrock upon which we can stand when buffeted by questions that cut to the core of our existence.

The freedom to choose. The freedom to choose is one of the rules of creation upon which this world was based. According to Doctrine and Covenants 93:30, intelligence is "independent in that sphere in which God has placed it, to act for itself. . . . Otherwise there is no existence." In addition, we read in Helaman 14:30, "Ye are free; ye are permitted to act for yourselves; for behold, God hath given unto you a knowledge and he hath made you free."

Our ability to choose is mitigated by our circumstances, however. The combined influence of environment, health, education, genetic makeup, and other factors limits our arena of choice. Yet within that arena we can choose in favor of faith, health, wholeness, and love. As we continue to make appropriate choices and act upon them, the arena becomes ever larger. The ability to choose is thus an integral part of the growth process.

It is so important, in fact, that God himself supports us so that we may "live and move and do according to [our] own will"

156

(Mosiah 2:21). He does so, even when we choose to act in opposition to his will. This is a powerful indication of the importance of agency. It has equally powerful implication for the way we conduct ourselves in our relationships. It teaches us that there is no place in the eternal scheme of things for the use of force, coercion, manipulation, or any other means of making someone act against his will to fill someone's expectations. What do we use instead? The power of love.

The power of love. The scriptures tell us that "no power or influence can or ought to be maintained . . . , only by persuasion, by long-suffering, by gentleness and meekness, and by love unfeigned; . . . reproving betimes with sharpness, when moved upon by the Holy Ghost; and then showing forth afterwards an increase of love toward him whom thou hast reproved . . . ; that he may know that thy faithfulness is stronger than the cords of death" (D&C 121:41–44).

Love is the most powerful force in the universe. The statement sounds trite, but scripture and the experiences of seekers throughout the centuries support it. The single greatest commandment is to love God, others, and ourselves (see Matt. 22:37–39; John 13:34), for love is a great power in the service of good. Love can transform. Love can heal.

Dostoevski had a vision of the power of love to heal and transform. He wrote: "I have seen it, *seen* it, and the living image of it has filled my soul forever. In one day, one hour, everything could be arranged at once! The chief thing is to love."[2]

So many of us seek to change ourselves and others by negative means. We cajole. We bribe. We criticize and condemn. We manipulate and control. None of these results in permanent change for the better. In fact, they create an atmosphere of fear, which limits rather than encourages growth. On the other hand, unconditional love creates an atmosphere in which the soul can expand. When we are free of fear, we can see more clearly. New avenues of action open up, new choices present themselves.

As we begin to take our first steps toward healing, we think of these principles primarily in regard to their effect on us personally. But as we continue to progress, we begin to see that they must apply to all. This realization forces us to take a critical look at the way we relate to our families, friends, and colleagues, and beyond that to how we relate to the cashier, the driver in front of us, and stranger on the street. We begin to ask ourselves some of the following questions:

- Do I see others as stereotypes of certain attributes or as individuals of eternal worth?

- Do I allow those around me the freedom to make their own choices, or do I try to force my preferences on them by controlling or manipulative behavior?

- Do I seek first to love others, or do I attempt first to change them into something I deem lovable?

In the eternities, relationships — including those in eternal families and celestial society — will be built upon these principles. The family that strives, however imperfectly, to implement them will reflect to some degree what is possible in the eternities.

Gospel-based Principles of Healing

Not only does the gospel teach principles of human relationships, it teaches principles of healing. The essence of the gospel is healing, or the Atonement. The gospel provides the necessary tools of faith, repentance, and the gift of the Holy Ghost to heal the separation resulting from the Fall.

How do these tools contribute to healing? Faith in the mission of Christ allows us to hope, and that hope gives us the courage to get up each morning and try again, sometimes in the face of seemingly insurmountable obstacles. The process of repentance gives us a way to harness the power of the Atonement and deal appropriately with guilt. It frees us of guilt's burden, opening us to the mercy and love of God, and encouraging us to be merciful and loving to others. The gift of the Holy Ghost blesses us with an ever-present guide who will teach, direct, and bring to remembrance things once learned at the feet of God.

The ordinances of the gospel provide us the means by which we bring the power of these principles into our lives. Baptism gives us the opportunity to enter into the path of healing through a covenant with our Father in Heaven. Partaking of the sacrament thoughtfully and worthily brings the power of the Spirit into our lives on a regular basis. It also helps us to remain humble and receptive. Receiving the gift of the Holy Ghost by the laying on of hands creates a unique relationship between the individual and this member of the Godhead.

The institution of the Church offers us the opportunity to enter into these ordinances. It provides us a forum in which to actualize our spirituality. It provides programs that support our personal and family goals and a social structure in which our chosen way of life is validated. Whatever difficulties individuals face, even including difficulties arising from member teachings or LDS cultural values, they can be addressed and worked through within the context of the gospel and the Church.

Transcendent Living

The hope that the gospel gives us all is that through our own efforts, the guidance of the Spirit, the power of the Atonement, and the love of God, we will be able to transcend the natural-man behaviors that have bound us in sorrow.

What will our lives look like when we begin to approach that state? Probably not much different from the way they look now. We will still have to earn a living, keep our homes clean and repaired, go shopping, cook meals and clean up afterward, do the washing, care for others, and fill our Church callings. Such a life will *feel* different, however, for our actions will be motivated by trust in the mission of Christ, the principle of agency, the worth of souls, and love of God, self, and others.

Transcendent living is in some aspects harder than simply following the checklist. It requires us to be highly sensitive to ourselves and to the Spirit. It requires us to take the time for whatever practices keep us grounded or rooted in love and in Jesus Christ (see Eph. 3:17; Col. 2:7). As we strive to do those things, love will teach us a new way to live.

In *The Broken Covenant*, Kathy, who is at last on her way to recovery, says, "Love's imperatives are internal, and the Spirit is teaching me what those imperatives are."[3] It is my conviction that healing our dysfunctional relationships will bring us closer to this transcendent ideal, closer to living the law of love and ultimately closer to Zion: to being of one heart and one mind.

CONCLUSION

At the conclusion of this book, I would like to add one further caution. When people learn something new, they sometimes become totally caught up in it. They feel that because it is right for them, it must be right for everyone else. With great enthusiasm, they try to tell their families what they have discovered. The response is not always what they expect or desire. In fact, they may encounter not only resistance to their new knowledge, but also hostility. This is especially possible when beliefs or behaviors are being challenged.

If this book has created an awareness of negative behavior patterns in your family, you probably are anxious to embark on a program to modify them. I urge you to use caution. New information of a sensitive nature must be shared quietly, a little bit at a time. Even so, you will likely meet with resistance. In this case, trying to force family members into your new mode of thinking may be tempting. But that would be using dysfunctional methods to cure dysfunction. (In cases where physical or sexual abuse is present, taking the slow approach is not appropriate. Then quick and decisive action is called for.)

The place to start, as always, is with oneself. You may be thinking what I have thought many times, "Why am I the one

161

who has to change? Why can't someone else do it for once!"
The answer is simple. First, we can only change ourselves; second, there always is something we can and probably should
change! And one person making one change can start a ripple
that will ultimately profoundly affect many lives.

WHAT NEXT?

If portions of what you have read seem to apply to your situation, you may wish to do one or more of the following:

I. Seek help through
    A. Church Social Services
    B. Your health group, family physicians, or programs presented in your local hospital
    C. Local entities of the following groups (check phone book for local chapter offices):
        1. 12-step programs such as
           a. Alcoholics Anonymous
           b. Incest Survivors Anonymous
           c. Overeaters Anonymous
           d. Emotions Anonymous
           e. Adult Children of Dysfunctional Families
        2. Adults Molested as Children
           c/o Parents United
           P.O. Box 952
           San Jose, CA 95108

II.   Increase your understanding of family rules, roles, and dramas by

A. Talking to family members and writing down or tape-recording reoccuring events, arguments, and other patterns in family history

B. Becoming aware of unresolved conflict (unfinished business) in your immediate family

C. Taking courses designed to help participants develop new responses to old patterns

D. Reading books such as

1. The New Peoplemaking by Virginia Satir

2. The Games People Play by Eric Berne

III.   Identify your thought patterns by

A. Keeping a log of intense feelings and the thoughts preceding those feelings

B. Reading books such as

1. Feeling Good and The Feeling Good Handbook by David Burne.

2. Telling Yourself the Truth by William Backus and Marie Chapian.

3. The Handbook to Higher Consciousness by Kent Keys (Don't let the title spook you, it's a good book!)

IV.   Reformat your thought patterns with visualizations and affirmations by

A. Doing the exercises in

1. Creative Visualization by Shakti Gawain

2. Gathering Power through Insight and Love by Ken Keyes, Jr., Penny Keyes, and staff

3. Any of the books on reparenting listed in section V

V.   Become a better parent to your inner child and own children by
   A.   Nurturing yourself daily
   B.   Attending an Adult Children of Dysfunctional Families group
   C.   Reading and working with books such as
      1.   *The Child Within* and *Gift to Myself* by Charles Whitfield
      2.   *Growing Up Again: Parenting Ourselves, Parenting Our Children* by Jean Illsley Clark and Connie Dawson
      3.   *Becoming Your Own Parent* by Dennis Wholely

VI.   Establish better boundaries by
   A.   Keeping a journal to help you become aware of what you really think and feel
   B.   Learning how to state your wants and needs clearly by
      1.   Taking classes
      2.   Reading books such as
         a.   *Telling Each Other the Truth* by William Backus
         b.   *When I Say No, I Feel Guilty* by Manuel J. Smith

VII.   Learn better communications skills by
   A.   Attending appropriate classes, ones that concentrate on listening and interaction skills
   B.   Reading books such as
      1.   *Parent Effectiveness Training* by Thomas Gordon
      2.   *I'm OK, You're OK* by Thomas A. Harris

165

NOTES

INTRODUCTION
1. *Bradshaw On: The Family* (Deerfield Beach: Health Communications, Inc., 1988), 37.

CHAPTER 2
1. *Ensign*, July 1989, 7.
2. "The Silent Survivor—Defining Abuse," seminar, 1990 Brigham Young University Women's Conference.
3. Fact sheet, National Committee for Prevention of Child Abuse, July 1990.
4. Alfie Kohn, "Shattered Innocence," *Psychology Today*, February 1987, 54.
5. "A Tale of Abuse," *Newsweek*, December 12, 1988, 59.
6. YWCA statistics quoted by Representative Wayne Owens in Congressional Update, July 1991.
7. Linda Bradley, A *Study of Physical Discipline Practices in Relationship to the Legal Definition of Child Abuse: A Study of 100 Utah Valley Families' Discipline Practices*, unpublished Master of Social Work research project, Brigham Young University, 1983.
8. Tim B. Heaton, Kristen L. Goodman, and Thomas B. Holman, *In Search of a Peculiar People: Are Mormons Really Different?* unpub. ms., BYU.
9. Boyd C. Rollins and Yaw Oheneba-Sakyi, "Physical Violence in Utah Households," unpub. ms., BYU.
10. "The Silent Survivor."

CHAPTER 4
1. Raymond Corsini, *Current Psychotherapies* (Itasca: F. E. Peacock Publishers, Inc., 1979), 463.

2. *Peoplemaking* (Palo Alto, California: Science and Behavior Books, Inc., 1972), 2.

CHAPTER 5

1. See, for example, Melodie Beattie, *Codependent No More* (San Francisco: Harper-Hazelden, 1987), 37–41; Pia Mellody, *Facing Codependence: What It Is, Where It Comes from, How It Sabotages Our Lives* (San Francisco: Harper-SanFrancisco, 1989), 3–57.

2. In Dennis Wholely, *Becoming Your Own Parent: The Solution for Adult Children of Alcoholic and Other Dysfunctional Families* (New York: Doubleday, 1988), 34.

3. In Wholely, 207.

4. In Wholely, 221.

CHAPTER 6

1. *For Your Own Good* (New York: Farrar, Straus and Giroux, 1983), 59.

2. Miller, 59–60.

CHAPTER 7

1. *Healing the Child Within* (Deerfield Beach: Health Communications, Inc., 1987), 43.

CHAPTER 8

1. *Bradshaw On: The Family*, 6.

CHAPTER 9

1. *Man's Search for Meaning* (New York: Pocket Books, 1959), 158.

2. Ezra Taft Benson, "Beware of Pride," *Ensign*, May 1989, 4–7.

3. *Co-dependence, Misunderstood–Mistreated* (San Francisco: Harper and Row Publishers, Inc., 1986), 75.

CHAPTER 10

1. *Breaking the Chains: Understanding Religious Addiction and Religious Abuse* (Long Beach: Emmaus Publications, 1989), 100.

CHAPTER 11

1. *Co-Dependency—What It Is and How to Reduce It within a Gospel Context*, on cassette (Beaverton: Dr. John C. Turpin & Associates, 1989).

2. *Wives of Alcoholics* (Deerfield Beach: Health Communications, Inc., 1985).

3. "The Abuse of Women: An Interview with Jane," *Exponent II*, 14, no. 1 (1987): 3.

4. *Turning Points* (New York: Fawcett Crest, 1979), 108, 111.

CHAPTER 12

1. In Wholely, 28.

168

2. *Adult Children of Alcoholics* (Deerfield Beach: Health Communications, Inc., 1983, 1990), 4–5.

3. *Woman and the Power Within* (Salt Lake City: Deseret Book, 1991), 248.

CHAPTER 14

1. In *Wholely*, 202.

2. *On Death and Dying:* (New York: Collier Books, 1969).

CHAPTER 15

1. "Becoming a Survivor," in *Woman and the Power Within*, 259.

2. David Viscott, *The Language of Feelings* (New York: Pocket Books, 1976), 23–24.

CHAPTER 16

1. *Peoplemaking*, 17.

2. In *Wholely*, 216.

CHAPTER 17

1. "The Abuse of Women," 3.

2. Judy Dushku, "Bishop, Please Believe My Story," *Exponent II*, 14, no. 1 (1987): 8.

3. B. Kent Harrison, comp. "LDS Church Statements, Quotes, and References on Abuse," April 1990, 1.

CHAPTER 20

1. "Consciousness of God: Supreme Goal of Life," *Improvement Era*, June 1967, 80.

CHAPTER 21

1. Roger Kallen and Randy K. Hardman, *Making Things Happen*, on cassette (Aurora: Human Development Institute, Inc., 1989).

2. Fyodor Dostoyevski, as quoted in Marilyn Ferguson, *The Aquarian Conspiracy* (Los Angeles: J. P. Tarcher, Inc., 1980), 402.

3. Carroll Hofeling Morris, *The Broken Covenant* (Salt Lake City: Deseret Book Company, 1985), PAGE.

REFERENCES FOR ADDITIONAL READING

Bass, Ellen, and Laura David. *The Courage to Heal*. New York: Harper & Row, 1988.

Beatty, Melody. *Codependent No More*. San Francisco: Harper-Hazelden, 1987.

Beatty, Melody. *Beyond Codependency*. San Francisco: Harper-Hazelden, 1989.

Beck, John C., and Martha Nibley Beck. *Breaking the Cycle of Compulsive Behavior*. Salt Lake City: Deseret Book Company, 1990.

Bednar, Richard L., and Scott R. Peterson. *Spirituality and Self-Esteem: Developing the Inner Self*. Salt Lake City: Deseret Book, 1990.

Benson, Ezra Taft. "Beware of Pride." *Ensign*, May 1989, 4–7.

Booth, Leo. *Breaking the Chains: Understanding Religious Addiction and Religious Abuse*. Long Beach: Emmaus Publications, 1989.

Bradshaw, John. *Bradshaw On: The Family*. Deerfield Beach: Health Communications, Inc., 1988.

Bradshaw, John. *Bradshaw On: Healing the Shame That Binds You*. Deerfield Beach: Health Communications, Inc., 1988.

Britsch, R. Lanier, and Terrance D. Olson, eds. *Counseling: A Guide to Helping Others, Volume 1*. Salt Lake City, Deseret Book, 1983.

———. *Counseling, Volume 2*. 1985.

Burns, David D. *Feeling Good: The New Mood Therapy*. New York: Signet Books, 1980.

Brown, Victor L., Jr. *Healing Troubled Relationships*. Salt Lake City: Bookcraft, 1989.

171

REFERENCES

Clark, Jean Illsley, and Connie Dawson. *Growing Up Again: Parenting Ourselves, Parenting Our Children.* San Francisco: Harper-Hazelden, 1989.

Dushku, Judy. "Bishop, Please Believe My Story." *Exponent II*, 14, no. 1 (1987).

Harris, Thomas A. *I'm OK—You're OK.* New York: Avon Books, 1969.

Horton, Ann L. "Women of Faith in a Violent World." In *A Heritage of Faith: Talks Selected from the BYU Women's Conference.* (Salt Lake City: Deseret Book, 1988), 100–109.

Horton, Anne L., and Judith A. Williamson. *Abuse and Religion.* Lexington: Lexington Books, 1988.

Mellody, Pia. *Facing Codependence: What It Is, Where It Comes from, How It Sabotages Our Lives.* San Francisco: HarperSanFrancisco, 1989.

Miller, Alice. *For Your Own Good.* New York: Farrar, Straus and Giroux, 1983.

Peterson, H. Burke. "Unrighteous Dominion." *Ensign*, July 1989, 7–11.

Satir, Virginia. *Peoplemaking.* Palo Alto: Science and Behavior Books, Inc. 1972.

"The Abuse of Women: An Interview with Jane." *Exponent II*, 14, no. 1 (1987).

The Twelve Steps for Everyone. Minneapolis: CompCare Publications, 1975.

Turpin, John C. *The New Stress Reduction for Mormons.* Salt Lake City: Covenant Communications, 1991.

Wholely, Dennis. *Becoming Your Own Parent: The Solution for Adult Children of Alcoholic and Other Dysfunctional Families.* New York: Doubleday, 1988.

Woititz, Janet G. *Adult Children of Alchoholics.* Deerfield Beach: Health Communications, Inc., 1990.